Practice Test
for the
CogAT®
GRADE 3 LEVEL 9
FORM 7 & 8

Copyright © 2019 by Origins Publications

Written and Edited by:
Gifted and Talented Test Preparation Team

ISBN: 978-1-948255-52-3

Origins Publications
New York, NY, USA

Email:info@originspublications.com

BONUS

DOWNLOAD QUANTITATIVE CHALLENGE QUESTIONS

If you also want additional quantitative challenge questions, please go to the following link to download them!

To get your challenge questions today, please visit:
https://originstutoring.lpages.co/cogat3challengequestions/

Challenge questions can help a student get used to doing the most difficult questions on the test.

Get the questions now at
https://originstutoring.lpages.co/cogat3challengequestions/

Origins Publications

Origins Publications helps students develop their higher-order thinking skills while also improving their chances of admission into gifted and accelerated-learner programs.

Our goal is to unleash and nurture the genius in every student. We do this by offering educational and test prep materials that are fun, challenging and provide a sense of accomplishment.

Please contact us with any questions.

info@originspublications.com

Contents

Introduction to the CogAT®

This book offers an overview of the types of questions on the CogAT® Level 9, test-taking strategies to improve performance, sample questions, and a full-length practice CogAT that students can use to assess their knowledge and practice their test-taking skills. It is important that you read this entire introduction!

Who Takes the CogAT® Level 9?

There are ten CogAT levels, which are based on age. The CogAT Level 9 (Form 7) was made for 9 year olds, and is often used as an assessment tool or admissions test in 3rd grade for entry into 3rd/4th grade of gifted and talented (GATE) programs and highly-competitive schools.

The CogAT Level 9 is also used as an assessment tool by teachers to figure out which students would benefit from an accelerated or remedial curriculum.

When Does the CogAT® Take Place?

This depends on the school district you reside in or want to attend. Check with the relevant school/district to learn more about test dates and the application/ registration process.

CogAT® Level 9 Overview

The CogAT is a group-administered test that features three independent 'batteries': Verbal, Quantitative, and Nonverbal. It is designed to assess learned reasoning in these three areas, which experts believe are the areas most closely linked to academic achievement. One, two, or all three batteries may be administered based on the specific needs of the test user. The test is timed, so a student's stress management and time management skills are also tested during the exam.

The CogAT covers topics that students may not see in school, so kids will need to think a little differently in order to do well.

Length

Students are given about 30 minutes to complete ONE battery in the CogAT Level 9 test. Children taking the Level 9 can be given each battery separately or all at the same time. A test administrator provides directions and controls pacing throughout the test. Including administration time, the CogAT 9 (all three batteries) will take between approximately 2.5-3 hours.

Format

The entire test (with three batteries) is made up of 170 multiple choice questions. The questions are distributed as follows:

Verbal Battery		Quantitative Battery	
Sentence Completion	20	Number Analogies	18
Verbal Classifications	20	Number Series	18
Verbal Analogies	22	Number Puzzles	16
Non-Verbal Battery			
Figure Matrices	20		
Figure Classification	20	Total Questions 170	
Paper Folding	16		

Test Sections

The test consists of verbal, nonverbal material and quantitative material.

VERBAL BATTERY

The verbal battery on the CogAT® is designed to measure a student's vocabulary, memory, ability to solve verbal problems, and ability to determine word relationships.

This battery has three question types (subtests).

- ✓ Sentence Completion: Students select the word that best completes the sentence.
- ✓ Verbal Classification: Students are given a series of three words that are in some way similar. The student then selects a word from the answer choices that is connected to the other three.
- ✓ Verbal Analogies: Students are provided with two words that form a pair, as well as a third word. From the answer choices, the student must select the word that goes with the third provided word.

In the verbal battery, the student must read individual words on two subtests (Verbal Analogies & Verbal Classification) and a sentence on one subtest (Sentence Completion).

NONVERBAL BATTERY

On the nonverbal battery, students are tested on their ability to reason using geometric shapes and figures. Students must use strategies to solve unique problems that they may never have encountered in school.

The nonverbal battery is composed of three question types (subtests):

- ✓ Figure Classification: Students are provided with three figures and must select the fourth figure that completes the set.
- ✓ Figure Matrices: Students are given a 2x2 matrix with the image missing in one cell. Students must determine the relationship between the two spatial forms in the top row and find a fourth image that has the same relationship to the spatial form in the bottom row.
- ✓ Paper Folding: Students must determine how a hole-punched, folded paper will look once it is unfolded.

QUANTITATIVE BATTERY

The quantitative battery measures abstract reasoning, quantitative reasoning, and problem solving skills.

The quantitative battery is composed of three question types (subtests):

- ✓ Number Series: Students are given a series of numbers (terms). Based on the terms in the series, students must determine what the next term in the series should look like.
- ✓ Number Puzzles: Students are asked to solve simple equations by finding a missing value.
- ✓ Number Analogies: Students are provided with two sets of analogous numbers, and a third set with a missing number. To determine the missing number, students must find the relationship between the numbers in each of the first two sets, and apply it to the final set.

Part 2: How to Use this Book

The CogAT is an important test and the more a student is familiar with the questions on the exam, the better she will fare when taking the test.

This book will help your student get used to the format and content of the test so s/he will be adequately prepared and feel confident on test day.

Inside this book, you will find:

- Sample question for each question type on the test and teaching tips to help your student approach each question type strategically and with confidence.

- Full-length CogAT® Level 9 practice test.

Part 3. Test Prep Tips and Strategies

Firstly, and most importantly, commit to make the test preparation process a stress-free one. A student's ability to keep calm and focused in the face of challenge is a quality that will benefit her throughout her academic life.

Be prepared for difficult questions from the get-go! There will be a certain percentage of questions that are very challenging for all children (or all ages for that matter!). It is key to encourage students to use all strategies available when faced with challenging questions. And remember that a student can get quite a few questions wrong and still do very well on the test.

Before starting the practice test, go through the sample questions and read the teaching tips provided at the beginning of the book. They will help you guide your student as he or she progresses through the practice test.

The following strategies may also be useful as you help your student prepare:

Before You Start

Find a quiet, comfortable spot to work free of distractions. Show your student how to perform the simple technique of shading (and erasing) bubbles.

During Prep

If your student is challenged by a question, ask your student to explain why he or she chose a specific answer. If the answer was incorrect, this will help you identify where your student is stumbling. If the answer was correct, asking your student to articulate her reasoning aloud will help reinforce the concept.

Encourage your student to carefully consider all the answer options before selecting one. Tell him or her there is only ONE answer.

If your student is stumped by a question, she or he can use the process of elimination. First, encourage your student to eliminate obviously wrong answers to narrow down the answer choices. If your student is still in doubt after using this technique, tell him or her to guess as there are no points deducted for wrong answers.

Review all the questions your student answered incorrectly, and explain to your student why the answer is incorrect. Have your student attempt these questions again a few days later to see if he now understands the concept.

Encourage your student to do her best, but take plenty of study breaks. Start with 10-15 minute sessions. Your student will perform best if she views these activities as fun and engaging, not as exercises to be avoided.

When to Start Preparing?

Every parent/teacher & student will approach preparation for this test differently. There is no 'right' way to prepare; there is only the best way for a particular student. We suggest students, at minimum, take one full-length practice test and spend 6-8 hours reviewing CogAT® practice questions.

If you have limited time to prepare, spend most energy reviewing areas where your student is encountering the majority of problems.

As they say, knowledge is power! Preparing for the CogAT® will certainly help your student avoid anxiety and make sure she does not give up too soon when faced with unfamiliar and perplexing questions.

CogAT® Verbal Battery
Sample Questions & Teaching Tips

This battery includes three types of questions.

i.   Sentence Completion
ii. Verbal Classifications
iii. Verbal Analogies

If your student/child is going to go through the battery as if s/he were taking it under real testing conditions, then you should allow 30 minutes to complete this battery.

Otherwise, we suggest that your student answers each question in his or her own time, while you guide, support and give feedback as s/he progresses. In this case, we also recommend that you spend a few minutes yourself reviewing the teaching tips for each section so you can be prepared to help your student if he or she struggles with a question.

Before starting the battery, have your student try the sample questions in the next few pages.

Sentence Completion

There are 20 Sentence Completion questions in the CogAT® Level 9.

SAMPLE QUESTION: Find the word that best completes the sentence.

The _____ of children are ready to take the test. They have all been preparing for weeks and know the material very well.

    A. majority   B. most   C. rest   D. minority   E. intelligent

Correct Answer: A. The word 'majority' is the best word as it relates to most of the children who have 'all been preparing for weeks and know the material very well.'

TEACHING TIPS

- Encourage your student to carefully read the sentence in order to understand its meaning and structure before moving on the answer choices.
- Ask your student to try to predict what word could be used in the sentence.
- Encourage your student to identify 'clue' words/phrases. These words can help point a student towards the correct answer. For example, "however" or "but" indicates the second part of the sentence will be a limitation, while words like "furthermore" mean further support or elaboration on a point.

Verbal Classifications

There are 20 Verbal Classifications questions in the CogAT® Level 9.

SAMPLE QUESTION: How are the three words in the top row related? Pick a word from the answer choices that belongs in the same group as the words in the top row.

basement   **attic**   **kitchen**

A. downstairs   **B. roof**   **C. garden**   **D. house**   **E. dining room**

Correct Answer: **E.** The similarity among the items is that they are all rooms in a house.

TEACHING TIPS

These questions test a student's ability to identify and classify common objects into basic categories by one or more common physical property or attribute. They also test knowledge of common objects and categories. Introduce these categories and characteristics in real-life situations and discuss the relationships between concepts with your student.

- Objects: Tools, stationary, musical instruments, kitchen instruments, land and air transportation objects.
- Animals: Birds, insects, sea or land animals, animal homes, animal babies
- Fruits, vegetables and spices
- Feelings/emotions
- States, Continents, Countries
- Professions. Sports
- Grammatical constructs: nouns, verbs, adjectives, adverbs.
- Elements in nature. Shapes

Encourage your student to expand on his knowledge of a category in a question. Ask him to name other objects that share the same characteristics and belong to a specific category.

Ask your student to explain why she chose a specific answer. This will help you identify where your student is stumbling or provide the opportunity to reinforce understanding of a category and the object/s that can "belong" to it.

Verbal Analogies

There are 22 Verbal Analogies questions in the CogAT® Level 9.

SAMPLE QUESTION: Find the relationship between the first two words, then choose a word that has the same relationship with the third word.

teacher : student   as   doctor :

A. hospital   B. patient   C. passenger   D. medicine   E. customer

Correct Answer: **B.** A teacher helps students as a doctor helps patients.

TEACHING TIPS

- To master analogies, a student needs to have general background knowledge, and an understanding/recognition of various relationships, including:

  → Object/function — One word in a pair describes the purpose or function of the other word.

  → Agent (person or animal)/location.

  → Agent (person or animal)/action.

  → Definition/Evidence—One word in a pair helps to define the other word; or, one word in a pair is a defining characteristic of the other word.

  → Synonym/Antonym—One word in a pair is a synonym or antonym of the other word.

  → Degree/Intensity—Both words in a pair are similar in concept, but vary in intensity.

  → Component/Part—One word in a pair represents one part of the other word, which represents a whole; or, one word is simply a component of the other.

- As often as possible, incorporate discussions about similarities, differences, and relationships between words into your everyday conversation with your student. Help your student begin thinking about how different words and concepts are connected to one another.

- When answering practice questions, teach your student to determine the relationship between the first pair of words before looking at the answer choices. Once your student determines the relationship between the first pair, she can then look at the answer choices to find the pair with the exact same relationship.

CogAT® Nonverbal Battery
Sample Questions & Teaching Tips

This battery includes three types of questions.

i. Figure Classifi ation
ii. Figure Matrices
iii. Paper Folding

If your student/child is going to go through the battery as if s/he were taking it under real testing conditions, then you should allow 30 minutes to complete this battery.

Otherwise, have your student answer each question in his or her own time, while you guide, support and give feedback as she progresses. Spend a few minutes reviewing the teaching tips for each section so you help your student if he struggles with a question.

Before starting the battery, ask your student to try the sample questions in the next few pages.

Figure Classification

There are 20 Figure Classification questions in the CogAT® Level 9.

SAMPLE QUESTION:

Look at the shapes in the top row. These shapes go together in a certain way. Which shape in the bottom row belongs with the shapes in the top row?

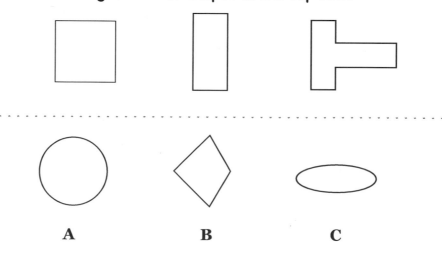

A   B   C

Correct Answer: **B.** In the top row, the three figures go together because all the shapes are made of straight lines. Your student needs to find the figure among the answer options that goes together with the shapes in the top row. Option A and C are incorrect because these shapes do not have straight lines. Option B is correct as this is the only shape that has straight lines like the shapes in the top row.

TEACHING TIPS

- After your student has answered the question, encourage her to expand on her knowledge of the category in the question.

- Ask him to name or draw other objects that share the same characteristics and belong to a specific category.

- Ask your student to explain why she chose a specific answer. This will help you identify where your student is stumbling or provide the opportunity to reinforce understanding of a category and the object/s that can "belong" to it.

Figure Matrices

There are 20 Figure Matrices questions in the CogAT® Level 9.

SAMPLE QUESTION:

Look at the shapes in the boxes on top. These shapes go together in a certain way. Which answer choice belongs where the question mark is?

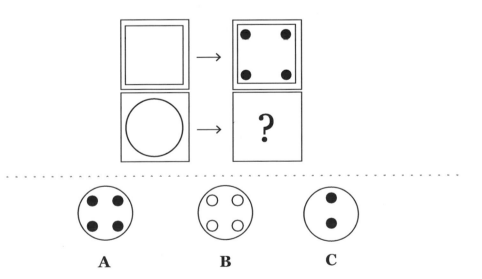

Correct Answer: **A.** In the top row, there are two figures that go together in a certain way. They go together in the sense that as the figure moves from left box to right box, it stays the same shape (a square) but adds four black circles inside.

Your student needs to find the figure among the answer options that fits best in the question mark box on the bottom row. The correct choice will have the same relationship with the figure on the bottom row that the figures in the top row have with each other.

Option B is incorrect because, although the figure is the same shape as the figure on the bottom row, the inside circles that are added are white. Option C is incorrect because, although the figure is the same shape as the figure on the bottom row, only two black inside circles are added. Option A is correct as the figure has the same shape (circle) as the figure on the bottom row and it has four black circles inside.

TEACHING TIPS

- Make sure your student knows key concepts that come up in these types of questions, including geometric concepts such as rotational symmetry, line symmetry, parts of a whole.

- If your student is finding these items difficult, encourage her to discover the pattern by isolating one element (e.g: outer shape, inner shape/s) and identify how it changes:

  → Ask: Is the color/shading of the element changing as it moves?

  → Ask: Is the element changing positions as it moves? Does it move up or down? Clockwise or counter-clockwise? Does it end up in the opposite (mirror) position?

  → Ask: Does the element disappear or increase in number as it moves along the row? Does it get bigger or smaller?

- Encourage your student to make a prediction for the missing object and compare the description with the answer choices.

Paper Folding

There are 16 Paper Folding questions in the CogAT® Level 9.

SAMPLE QUESTION:

The paper in the top row is folded and cut as shown. Which paper in the bottom row is the result when the paper is unfolded?

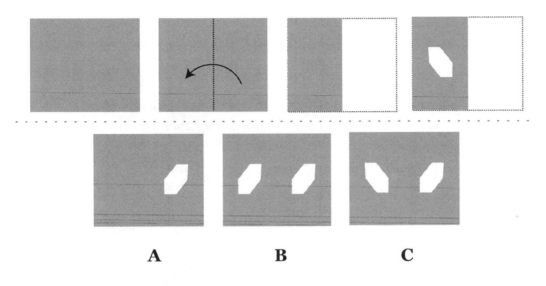

A   **B**   **C**

Correct Answer: C. In the top row, the paper is folded in half vertically. A shape is cut out of the folded paper. Your student needs to choose which answer option shows how the paper will look when unfolded. The correct choice will be an unfolded paper with two shapes cut out of it. The shape on the right will mirror the shape on the left. Option A is incorrect as it shows only one shape cut out from the paper. Option B is incorrect as both shapes are placed in the same direction and are not mirror images of each other. Option C is correct as the right shape reflects the left shape, like a mirror image.

TEACHING TIPS

In addition to using the written practice questions, a good way to prepare for this unique and challenging question type is through hands-on practice with real paper. For example, you can show your student that if a paper is folded once and a hole is punched into it, she will see two holes on either side of the fold once the paper is unfolded.

CogAT® Quantitative Battery
Sample Questions & Teaching Tips

This battery includes three types of questions.

i.   Number Series
ii. Number Puzzles
iii. Number Analogies

If your student/child is going to go through the battery as if s/he were taking it under real testing conditions, then you should allow 30 minutes to complete this battery.

Otherwise, have your student answer each question in his or her own time, while you guide and give feedback as s/he progresses. Spend a few minutes reviewing the teaching tips for each section so you can help your student if he struggles with a question.

Before starting the battery, have your student try the sample questions in the next few pages.

Number Series

There are 18 Number Series questions in the CogAT® Level 9.

SAMPLE QUESTION: Pick a number which follows the same rule as the order of numbers in the top row and replace the question mark with this number.

| 40 | 34 | 28 | 22 | 16 | 10 | ? |

| A. 6 | B. 4 | C. 16 | D. 8 | E. 2 |

Correct Answer: B. The rule is to subtract 6 from each term in the series, so the answer is 4 (option B).

TEACHING TIPS

Because your student may not have formal academic experience with this question type. it is important to practice working with many of these questions before the test. You can also find workbooks or games related to number patterns and sequences to help your child further his or her understanding of these concepts in an engaging manner.

Number Puzzles

There are 16 Number Puzzles questions in the CogAT® Level 9.

SAMPLE QUESTION: Replace the question mark with the correct number to solve the equation.

$$20 \quad + \quad ? \quad = \quad 5 \quad \times \quad 4$$

A. 5   B. 25   C. 0   D. 9   E. 20

Correct Answer: C. $20 + 0 = 5 \times 4$

TEACHING TIPS

- This question type requires your student to solve basic math equations, so practice with numbers and problem solving is essential.

- Make sure your student understands the meaning of "equal," since the object is to supply the missing piece of information that will make two provided equations equal to one another.

- You can also teach your student to approach the question by "plugging in" the answer choices and solving to see if the result is equal to the other equation in the question.

Number Analogies

There are 18 Number Analogies questions in the CogAT® Level 9.

SAMPLE QUESTION: Find the relationship between the numbers in the first set, and between the numbers in the second set. Then choose a number which follows the same pattern when paired with the number in the third set.

[10 → 2]   [20 → 4]   [30 → ?]

A. 3   B. 5   C. 6   D. 4   E. 10

Correct Answer: **C.** The rule is to divide the first number in each set by 5, so the answer is 6 (option C).

TEACHING TIPS

- Your student is probably not accustomed to completing number matrices, so it is important to frequently expose him to this question type in order to build confidence and familiarity.

- Show how to approach solving a number matrix by "thinking aloud" as you work through a question with your student.

- Work with your student on basic mathematical concepts, including addition, subtraction, division, multiplication.

COGAT®
PRACTICE TEST

VERBAL BATTERY

• •

VERBAL ANALOGIES

• •

For each item, the student is presented with two words that have a relationship or go together in a particular way.

The student needs to figure out the relationship between the first two words. The student then needs to choose the word in the answer choices that has the same relationship with the third word.

Harper

1. **candle : wax as window : ?**

    A. door   **B.** fabric   **C.** open   **D.** glass   **E.** plastic

2. ✗ **dog : mammal as frog : ?**

    A. slimy   **B.** amphibian   **C.** reptile   **D.** animal   **E.** toad

3. **football : field as tennis : ?**

    A. sport   **B.** track   **C.** ring   **D.** court   **E.** ball

4. **cotton : fabric as gold : ?**

    A. scarf   **B.** metal   **C.** umbrella   **D.** saucepan   **E.** wool

5. **desert : sand as lake : ?**

    A. blue   **B.** fish   **C.** cactus   **D.** boat   **E.** water

VERBAL ANALOGIES

6. rowboat : oar as car : ?

   A. door   **B.** road   **C.** drive   **D.** truck   **E.** steering wheel

7. spots : ladybug as stripes : ?

   A. leopard   **B.** tiger   **C.** elephant   **D.** stars   **E.** ant

8. rein : rain as there : ?

   A. them   **B.** rare   **C.** their   **D.** are   **E.** that

9. clock : time as ruler : ?

   A. distance   **B.** measure   **C.** inches   **D.** volume   **E.** numbers

10. teacher : student as doctor : ?

   A. hospital   **B.** patient   **C.** passenger   **D.** medicine   **E.** customer

VERBAL ANALOGIES

11. **three : triangle as eight : ?**

   A. square   **B.** shape   **C.** octagon   **D.** circle   **E.** pentagon

12. **pear : pair as hare : ?**

   A. rabbit   **B.** shoes   **C.** hair   **D.** hairy   **E.** hares

13. **nail polish : nails as earring : ?**

   A. diamond   **B.** beauty   **C.** ears   **D.** jewelry   **E.** lips

14. **I am : I'm as you are : ?**

   A. you're   **B.** yours   **C.** you'd   **D.** you   **E.** are

15. **bee : larva as fly : ?**

   A. baby   **B.** chrysalis   **C.** insect   **D.** tadpole   **E.** maggot

Gifted & Talented Test Prep Team

VERBAL ANALOGIES

16. **spider : web as wasp : ?**

    ✗ **A.** sting   **B.** hive   **C.** nest   **D.** pit   **E.** den

17. **amusing : hilarious as sad : ?**

    A. giggle   **B.** unacceptable   **C.** devastating   **D.** happy   **E.** hurt

18. **ring : finger as tie : ?**

    ✗ **A.** body   **B.** neck   **C.** suit   **D.** clothing   **E.** jewelry

19. **swift : leopard as slow : ?**

    A. rapid   **B.** lion   **C.** horse   **D.** snail   **E.** walk

20. ✗ **comb: hair as hammer: ?**

    A. nail   **B.** brush   **C.** tool   **D.** workshed   **E.** screwdriver

VERBAL ANALOGIES

21. **white : black as before : ?**

    A. over   **B.** color   **C.** advance   **D.** gray   **E.** after

22. **mansion : shack as yacht : ?**

    A. paddle   **B.** ocean   **C.** sail   **D.** dinghy   **E.** mobile

VERBAL BATTERY

• •

VERBAL CLASSIFICATIONS

• •

For each item, the student is presented with three words on the top row. The students needs to figure out how these words are related. :

The student then needs to pick a word from the answer choices that belongs in the same group as the three words in the top row.

VERBAL CLASSIFICATIONS

1. **comma   period   exclamation point**

    A. sentence   **B.** letters   **C.** vowels   **D.** question mark   **E.** paragraph

2. **cockpit   engine   wheels**

    A. wings   **B.** car   **C.** drive   **D.** stern   **E.** plane

3. **dog   cat   hamster**

    A. lion   **B.** elephant   **C.** beaver   **D.** camel   **E.** lizard

4. **pencil   marker   crayon**

    A. drawing   **B.** chalk   **C.** colors   **D.** design   **E.** sharpener

5. **oak   maple   willow**

    A. trees   **B.** pollen   **C.** acorn   **D.** birch   **E.** leaves

CogAT® Level 9 Test Prep Book   Gifted & Talented Test Prep Team

6.   **chicken   turkey   duck**

    A. guinea pig   **B.** dog   **C.** goose   **D.** birds   **E.** farm

7.   **basement   attic   kitchen**

    A. downstairs   **B.** roof   **C.** garden   **D.** house   **E.** dining room

8.   **Maryland   New York   Florida**

    A. state   **B.** cities   **C.** Maine   **D.** America   **E.** France

9.   **headphones   earrings   hearing-aids**

    A. jewelry   **B.** tiara   **C.** ear muffs   **D.** ears   **E.** hear

10.   **lens   pupil   cornea**

    A. iris   **B.** eye   **C.** anatomy   **D.** brainstorm   **E.** see

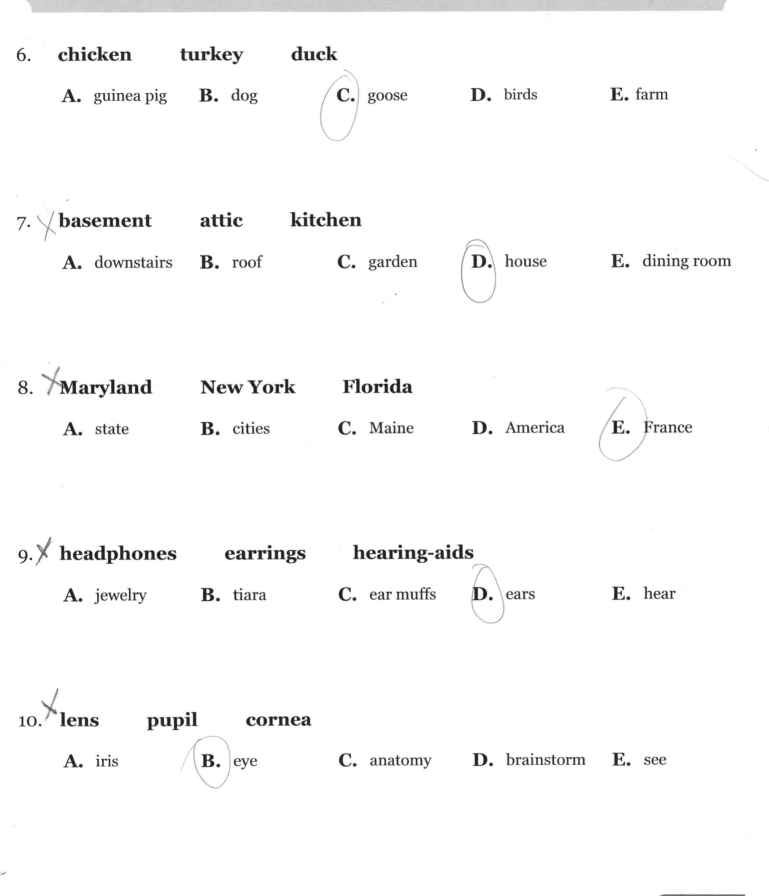

VERBAL CLASSIFICATIONS

11. **polka   waltz   rumba**

   A. dance   **B.** dots   **C.** tango   **D.** music   **E.** partner

12. **rectangle   square   rhombus**

   A. triangle   **B.** trapezoid   **C.** parallelogram   **D.** pentagon   **E.** octagon

13. **beside   under   above**

   A. hide   **B.** ran   **C.** in   **D.** desk   **E.** it

14. **that's   there's   he's**

   A. it's   **B.** you'll   **C.** she   **D.** is   **E.** they'd

15. **kangaroo   frog   rabbit**

   A. animals   **B.** grasshopper   **C.** hippo   **D.** penguin   **E.** rhino

VERBAL CLASSIFICATIONS

16. **bake   steam   grill**

   A. cook   **B.** food   **C.** burger   **D.** shop   **E.** roast

17. **science   music   history**

   A. achool   **B.** Spanish   **C.** American   **D.** lesson   **E.** recess

18. **and   since   so**

   A. word   **B.** it   **C.** go   **D.** how   **E.** but

19. **television   blender   car**

   A. trashcan   **B.** smoothie   **C.** items   **D.** cellphone   **E.** sofa

20. **Africa   cat   John**

   A. desk   **B.** meows   **C.** in   **D.** yet   **E.** the

VERBAL BATTERY

• •

SENTENCE COMPLETION

• •

For each item, the student is presented with a sentence that has a missing word.

The student needs to find the word from the answer choices that best completes the sentence.

SENTENCE COMPLETION

1. Sarah was worried when the lightning caused her dog to _tremble_ all over.

   A. growl   **B.** bark   **C.** tremble   **D.** frighten   **E.** roll

2. The teacher tried to _simplify_ the problem for her students by breaking it into smaller parts.

   A. create   **B.** simplify   **C.** understand   **D.** measure   **E.** teach

3. Our science project needs to be ready by Friday, so we better _____ our efforts.

   A. discuss   **B.** accelerate   **C.** stop   **D.** examine   **E.** experiment

4. John couldn't understand the lesson because the _mumbling_ teacher spoke too quietly.

   A. mumbling   **B.** regretful   **C.** clever   **D.** shouting   **E.** talkative

5. The cafeteria's fruit and vegetable bar encouraged _healthy_ eating.

   A. meat   **B.** suitable   **C.** healthy   **D.** unhealthy   **E.** food

CogAT® Level 9 Test Prep Book   Gifted & Talented Test Prep Team

SENTENCE COMPLETION

6. It took a long time for the man to move the *heavy* furniture into the house.

   A. plastic **B.** far-away **C.** solid **D.** kitchen **E.** heavy

7. An oaf is described as clumsy; a ballerina is described as _____.

   A. pretty **B.** dancing **C.** graceful **D.** falling **E.** bouncy

8. Ron loved to plant flowers, *but* he disliked watering them every week.

   A. and **B.** but **C.** moreover **D.** so **E.** when

9. I know the wooly mammoth is *extinct* because it no longer exists on the Earth.

   A. extinct **B.** tiny **C.** disappeared **D.** rare **E.** hidden

10. A pharmacist dispenses *medicine*.

   A. food **B.** patients **C.** chickens **D.** medicine **E.** tractors

SENTENCE COMPLETION

11. A pencil is filled with graphite.

   A. saucepan   **B.** pencil   C. pen   **D.** bucket   **E.** cement

12. Dante needs to take his medicine, so he can recover from his illness.

   A. run   **B.** rest   **C.** escape   **D.** choose   **E.** recover

13. I wanted to play baseball, and I found my bat and ran to the field.

   A. so   **B.** but   **C.** or   **D.** however   **E.** and

14. The pack of wolves included adults and their young.

   A. pack   **B.** herd   **C.** pod   **D.** school   **E.** bunch

15. My friends love the theater, however I prefer the movies.

   A. similarly   **B.** despite   **C.** secondly   **D.** therefore   **E.** however

SENTENCE COMPLETION

16. The _most_ of children are ready to take the test. They have all been preparing for weeks and know the material very well.

    A. majority   B. most   C. rest   D. minority   E. intelligent

17. The tree blossoms bloomed _earlier_ than expected.

    A. early   B. earlier   C. earliest   D. before   E. colorful

18. In our school, pop music is really popular. At recess, students are _often_ singing the latest hit songs.

    A. rarely   B. never   C. not   D. really   E. often

19. The boss _____ the employees when she talks too quickly, as they can't understand everything she says.

    A. enourages   B. silences   C. confuses   D. inspires   E. teaches

20. The homeless man was _grateful_ when he found a shelter to protect himself from the rain.

    A. discouraged   B. unhappy   C. grateful   D. kind   E. confused

NONVERBAL BATTERY

· · · · · · · · · · ·

FIGURE MATRICES

· ·

Harper 16

room 5

Figure Matrices

Look at the shapes in the boxes on top. These shapes go together in a certain way. Which shape belongs where the question mark is?

1

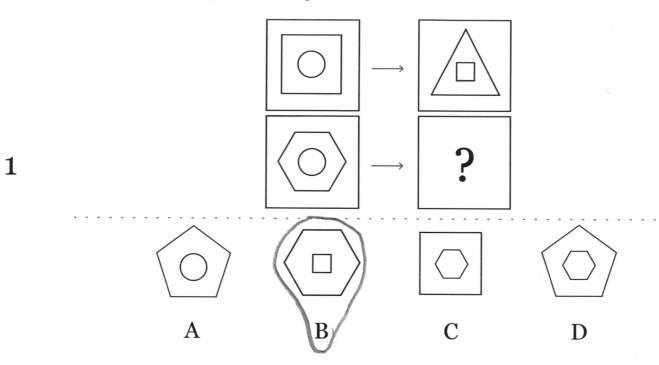

A   B   C   D

Look at the shapes in the boxes on top. These shapes go together in a certain way. Which shape belongs where the question mark is?

2

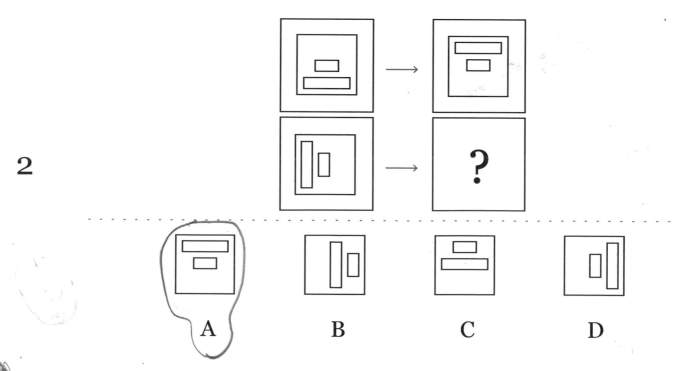

A   B   C   D

Look at the shapes in the boxes on top. These shapes go together in a certain way.
Which shape belongs where the question mark is?

3

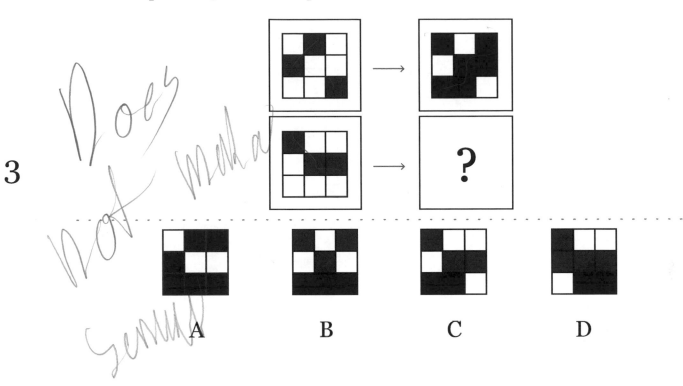

Look at the shapes in the boxes on top. These shapes go together in a certain way.
Which shape belongs where the question mark is?

4

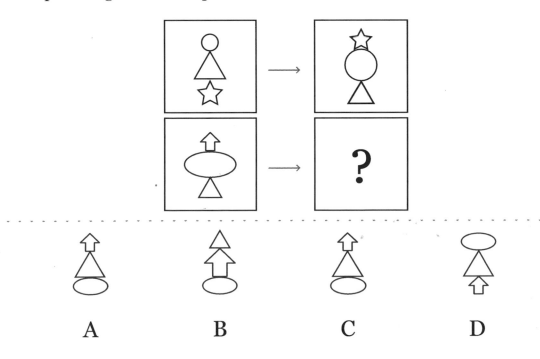

Figure Matrices

Look at the shapes in the boxes on top. These shapes go together in a certain way. Which shape belongs where the question mark is?

5

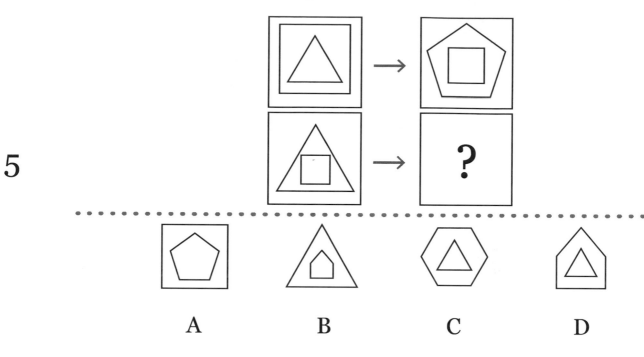

Look at the shapes in the boxes on top. These shapes go together in a certain way. Which shape belongs where the question mark is?

6

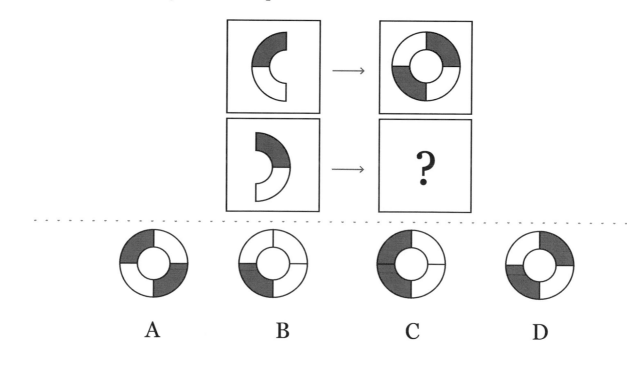

Figure Matrices

Look at the shapes in the boxes on top. These shapes go together in a certain way. Which shape belongs where the question mark is?

7

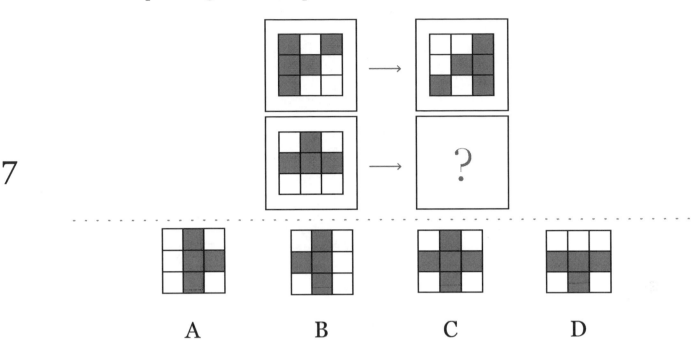

Look at the shapes in the boxes on top. These shapes go together in a certain way. Which shape belongs where the question mark is?

8

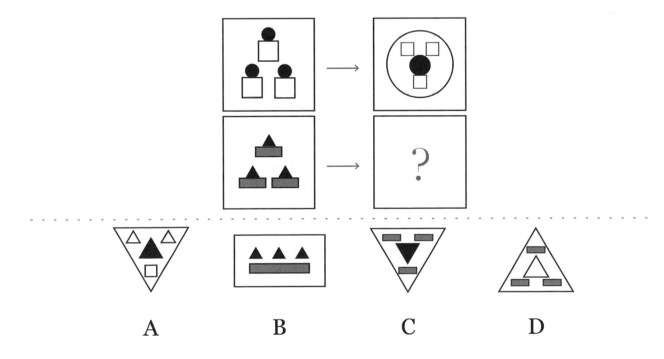

Look at the shapes in the boxes on top. These shapes go together in a certain way. Which shape belongs where the question mark is?

9

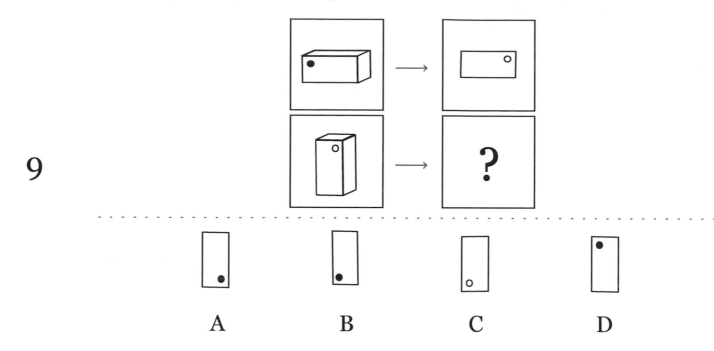

Look at the shapes in the boxes on top. These shapes go together in a certain way. Which shape belongs where the question mark is?

10

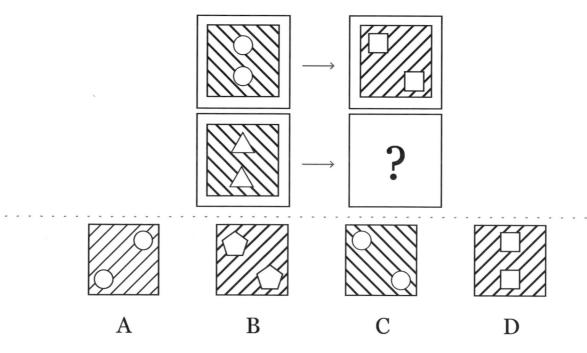

Figure Matrices

Look at the shapes in the boxes on top. These shapes go together in a certain way. Which shape belongs where the question mark is?

11

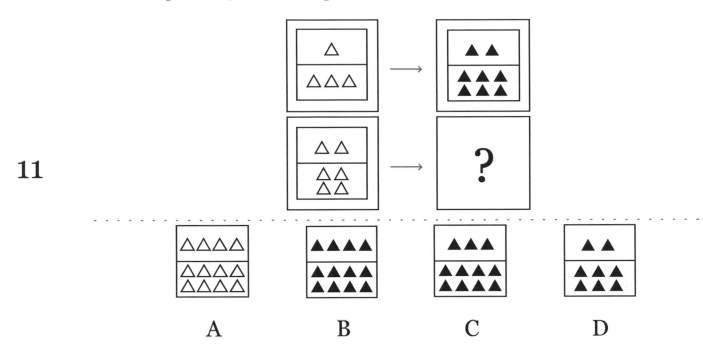

A   B   C   D

Look at the shapes in the boxes on top. These shapes go together in a certain way. Which shape belongs where the question mark is?

12

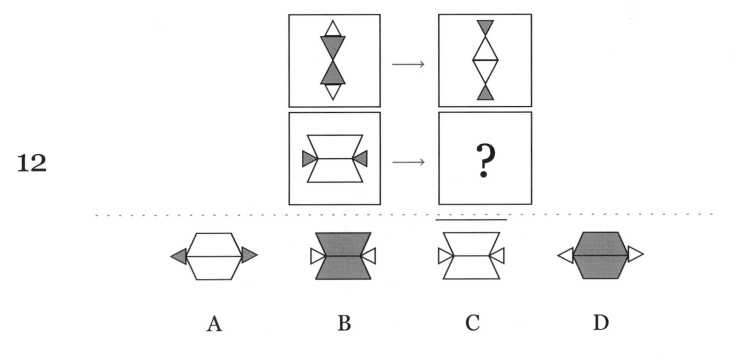

A   B   C   D

Look at the shapes in the boxes on top. These shapes go together in a certain way. Which shape belongs where the question mark is?

13

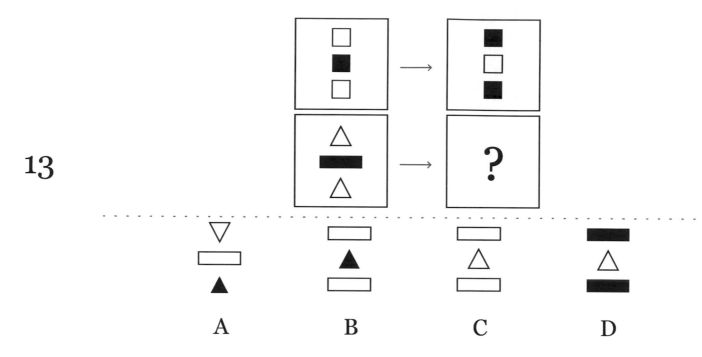

| A | B | C | D |

Look at the shapes in the boxes on top. These shapes go together in a certain way. Which shape belongs where the question mark is?

14

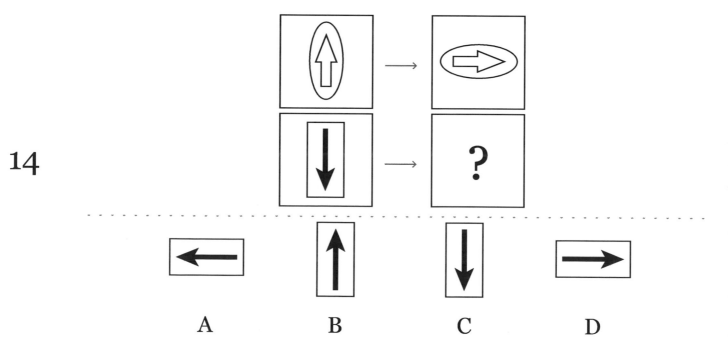

| A | B | C | D |

Figure Matrices

Look at the shapes in the boxes on top. These shapes go together in a certain way. Which shape belongs where the question mark is?

15

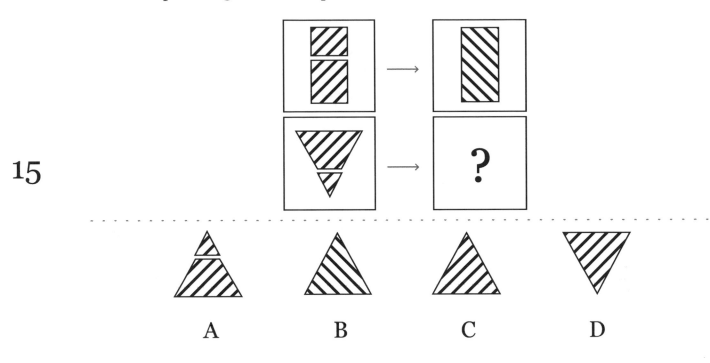

A   B   C   D

Look at the shapes in the boxes on top. These shapes go together in a certain way. Which shape belongs where the question mark is?

16

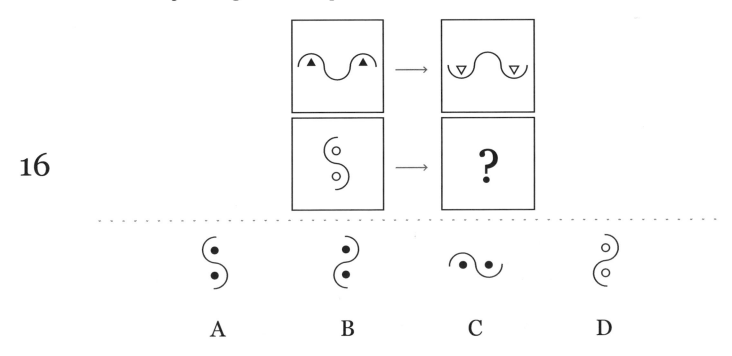

A   B   C   D

Look at the shapes in the boxes on top. These shapes go together in a certain way. Which shape belongs where the question mark is?

17

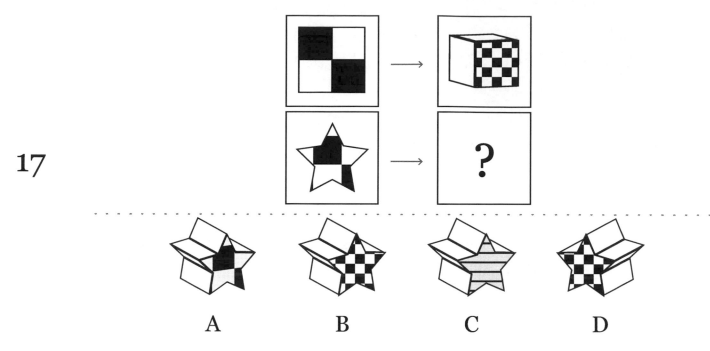

A   B   C   D

Look at the shapes in the boxes on top. These shapes go together in a certain way. Which shape belongs where the question mark is?

18

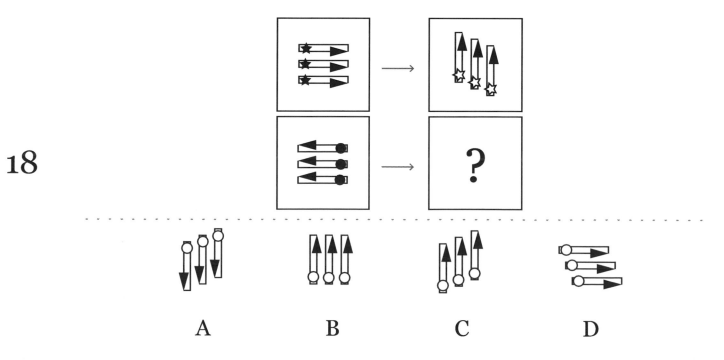

A   B   C   D

Figure Matrices

Look at the shapes in the boxes on top. These shapes go together in a certain way. Which shape belongs where the question mark is?

19

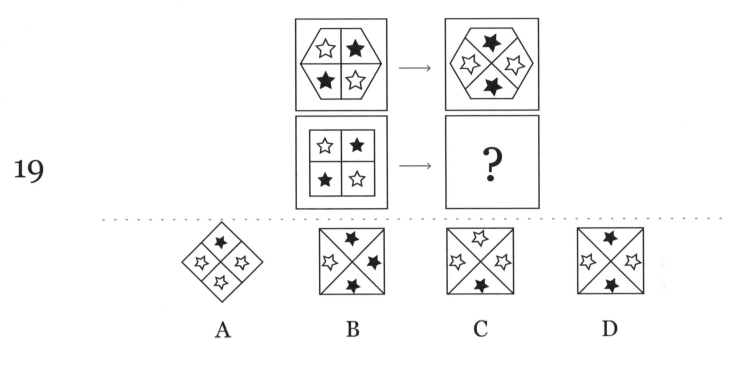

Look at the shapes in the boxes on top. These shapes go together in a certain way. Which shape belongs where the question mark is?

20

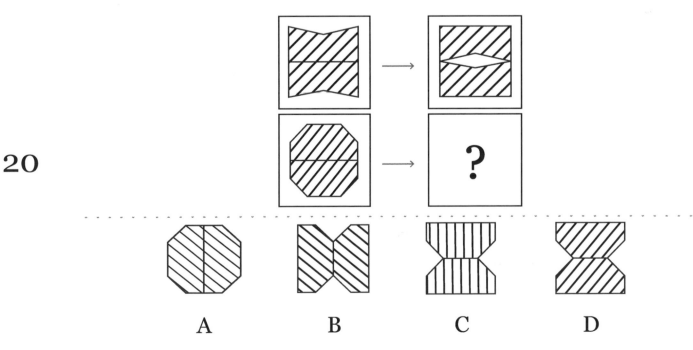

NONVERBAL BATTERY

• • • • • • • • • • • • •

FIGURE CLASSIFICATIONS

• •

Figure Classifications

Look at the shapes in the top row. These shapes go together in a certain way. Which shape in the bottom row belongs with the shapes in the top row?

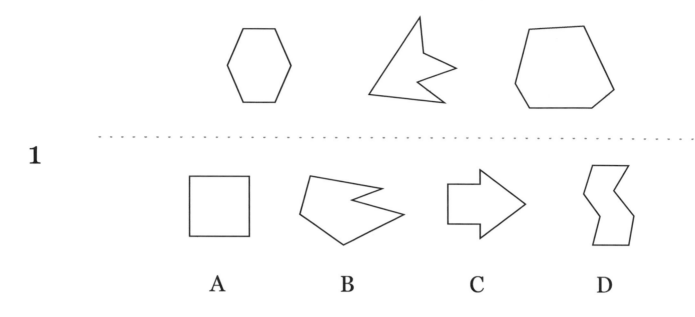

1

A   B   C   D

Look at the shapes in the top row. These shapes go together in a certain way. Which shape in the bottom row belongs with the shapes in the top row?

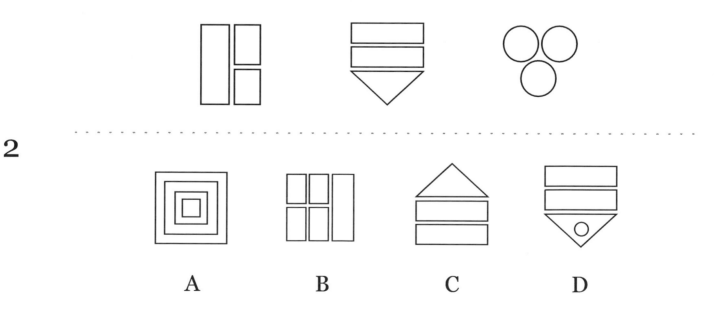

2

A   B   C   D

Figure Classifications

Look at the shapes in the top row. These shapes go together in a certain way. Which shape in the bottom row belongs with the shapes in the top row?

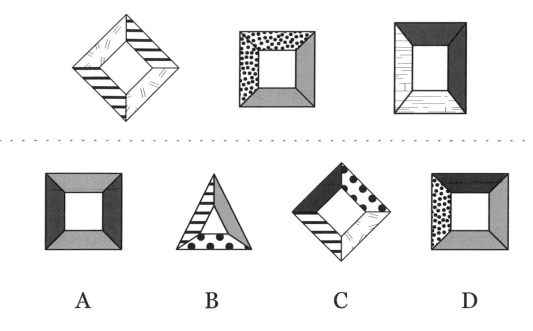

3

A   B   C   D

Look at the shapes in the top row. These shapes go together in a certain way. Which shape in the bottom row belongs with the shapes in the top row?

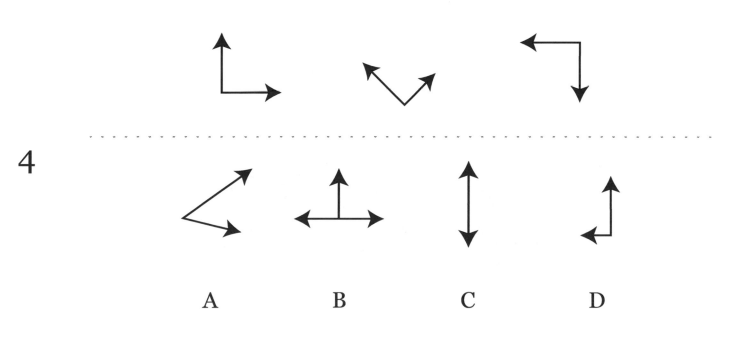

4

A   B   C   D

Look at the shapes in the top row. These shapes go together in a certain way. Which shape in the bottom row belongs with the shapes in the top row?

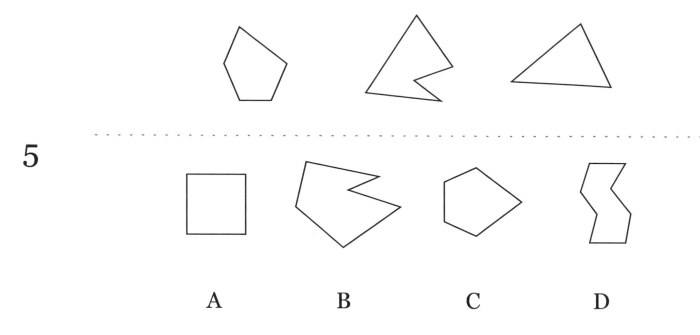

5

A   B   C   D

Look at the shapes in the top row. These shapes go together in a certain way. Which shape in the bottom row belongs with the shapes in the top row?

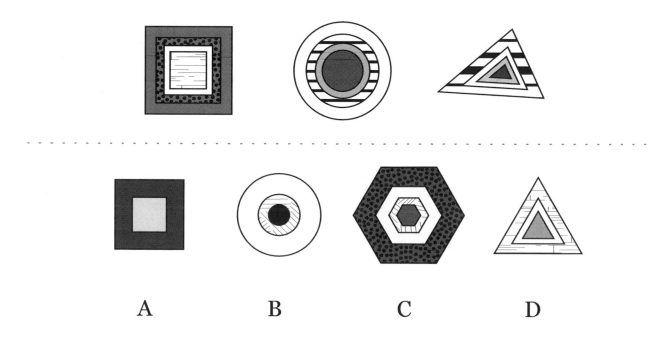

6

A   B   C   D

Look at the shapes in the top row. These shapes go together in a certain way. Which shape in the bottom row belongs with the shapes in the top row?

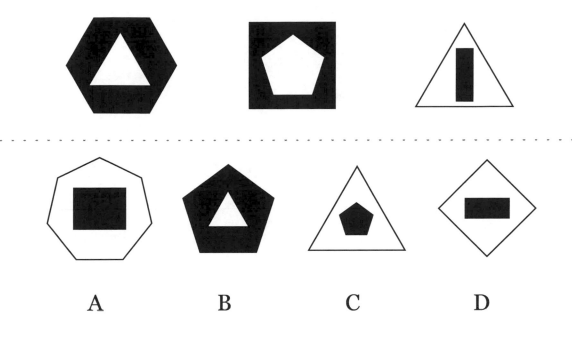

7

A   B   C   D

Look at the shapes in the top row. These shapes go together in a certain way. Which shape in the bottom row belongs with the shapes in the top row?

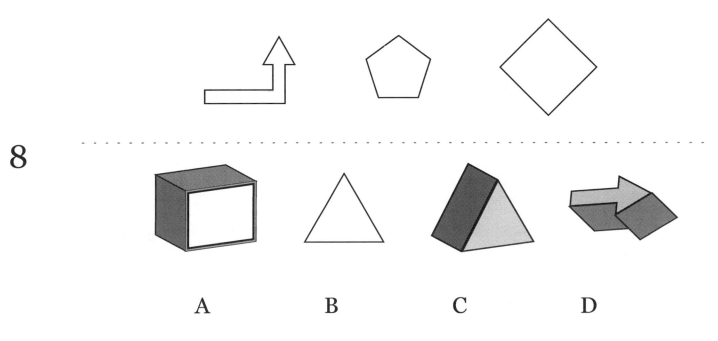

8

A   B   C   D

Look at the shapes in the top row. These shapes go together in a certain way. Which shape in the bottom row belongs with the shapes in the top row?

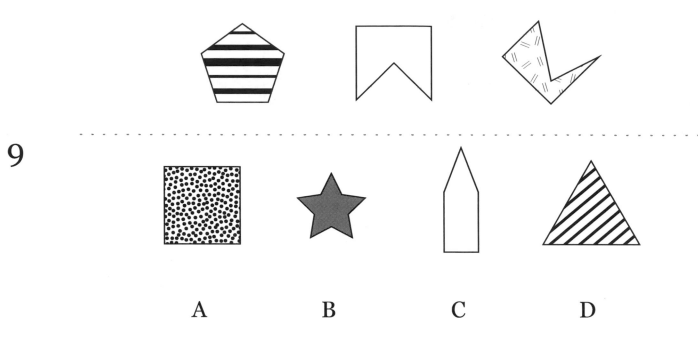

9

A	B	C	D

Look at the shapes in the top row. These shapes go together in a certain way. Which shape in the bottom row belongs with the shapes in the top row?

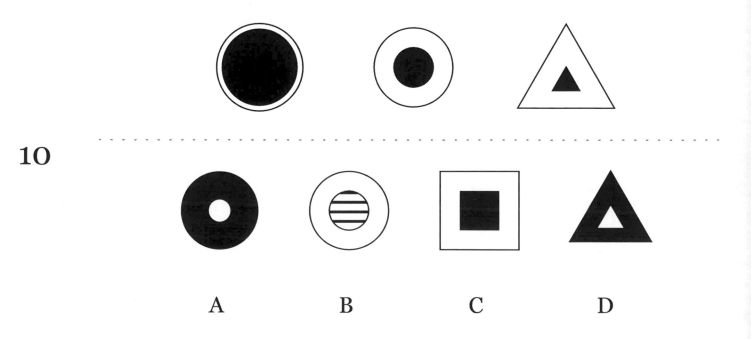

10

A	B	C	D

Look at the shapes in the top row. These shapes go together in a certain way. Which shape in the bottom row belongs with the shapes in the top row?

11

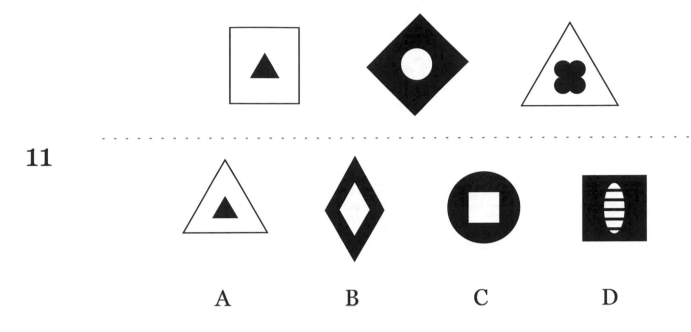

A   B   C   D

Look at the shapes in the top row. These shapes go together in a certain way. Which shape in the bottom row belongs with the shapes in the top row?

12

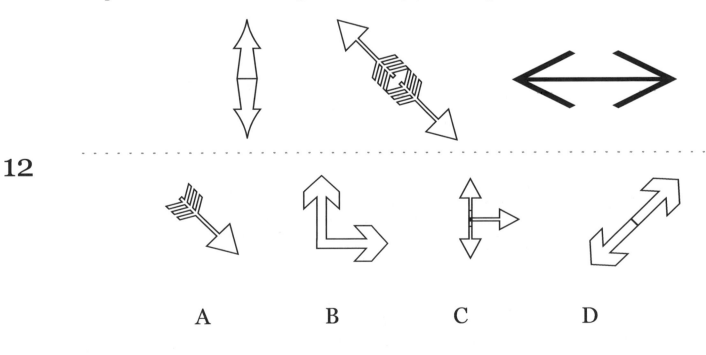

A   B   C   D

Figure Classifications

Look at the shapes in the top row. These shapes go together in a certain way. Which shape in the bottom row belongs with the shapes in the top row?

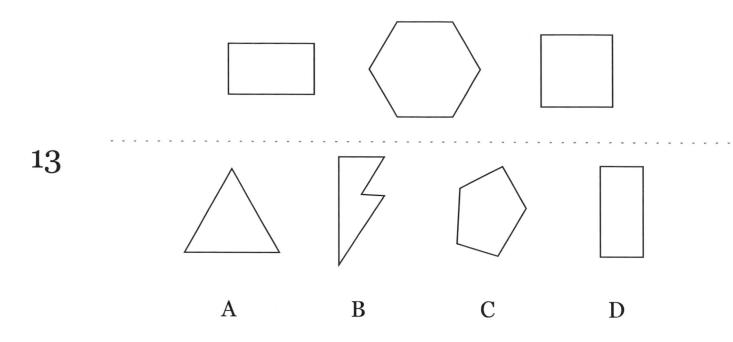

13

A   B   C   D

Look at the shapes in the top row. These shapes go together in a certain way. Which shape in the bottom row belongs with the shapes in the top row?

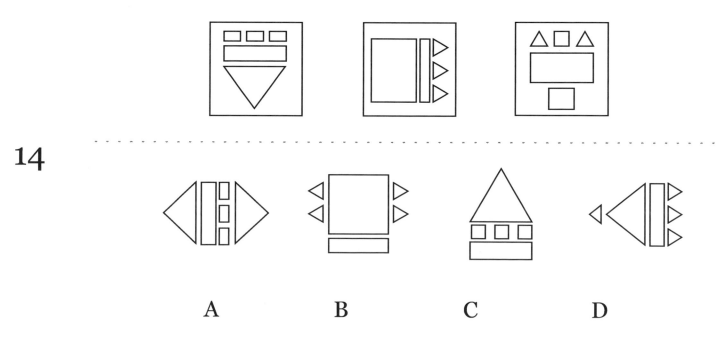

14

A   B   C   D

Gifted & Talented Test Prep Team

Look at the shapes in the top row. These shapes go together in a certain way. Which shape in the bottom row belongs with the shapes in the top row?

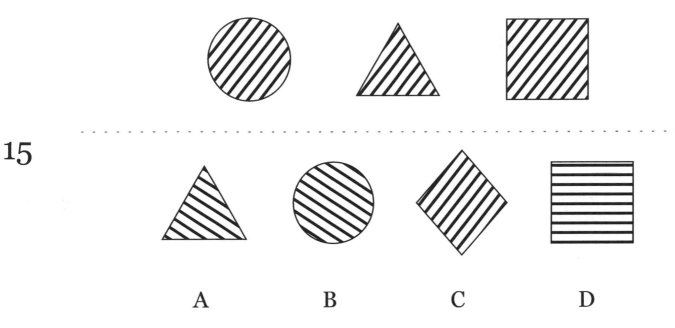

15

Look at the shapes in the top row. These shapes go together in a certain way. Which shape in the bottom row belongs with the shapes in the top row?

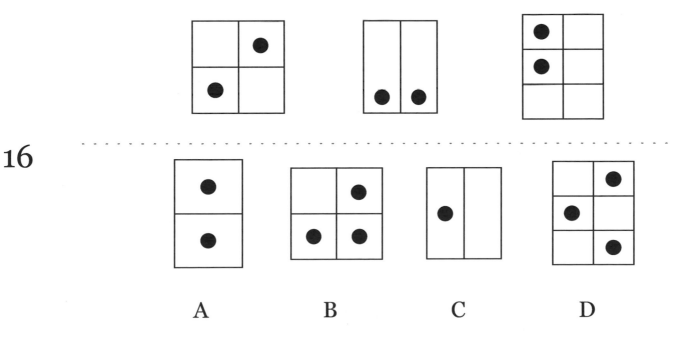

16

Figure Classifications

Look at the shapes in the top row. These shapes go together in a certain way. Which shape in the bottom row belongs with the shapes in the top row?

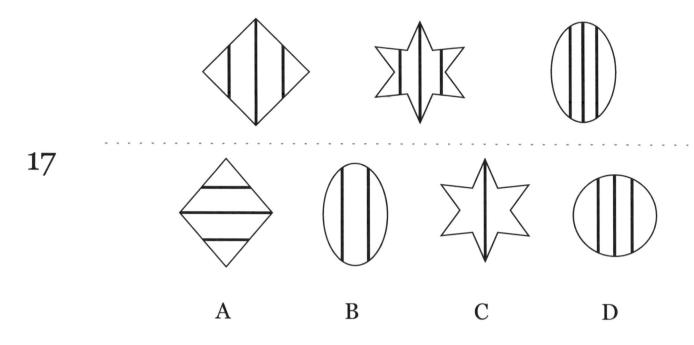

17

A   B   C   D

Look at the shapes in the top row. These shapes go together in a certain way. Which shape in the bottom row belongs with the shapes in the top row?

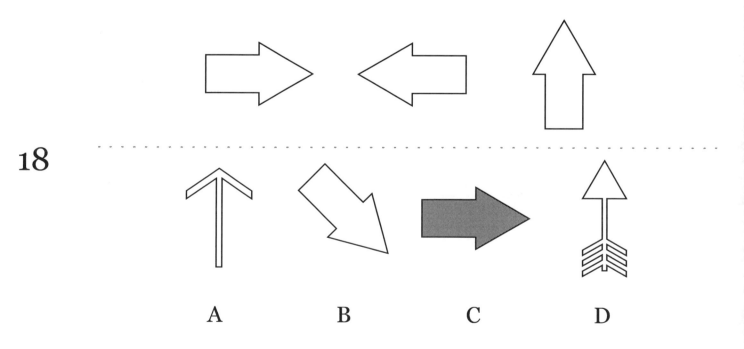

18

A   B   C   D

CogAT® Level 9 Test Prep Book   Gifted & Talented Test Prep Team

Look at the shapes in the top row. These shapes go together in a certain way. Which shape in the bottom row belongs with the shapes in the top row?

19

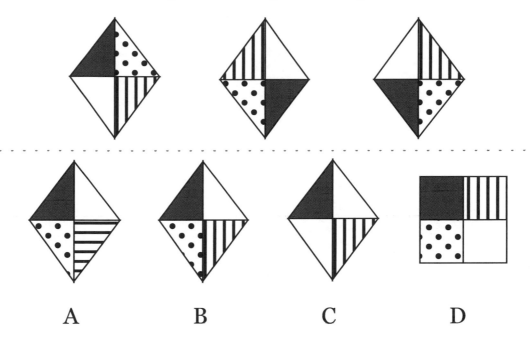

A   B   C   D

Look at the shapes in the top row. These shapes go together in a certain way. Which shape in the bottom row belongs with the shapes in the top row?

20

A   B   C   D

NONVERBAL BATTERY

• • • • • • • • • • • • •

PAPER FOLDING

• • • • • • • • • • • • • • • • • • •

The paper in the top row is folded and cut as shown. Which paper in the bottom row is the result when the paper is unfolded?

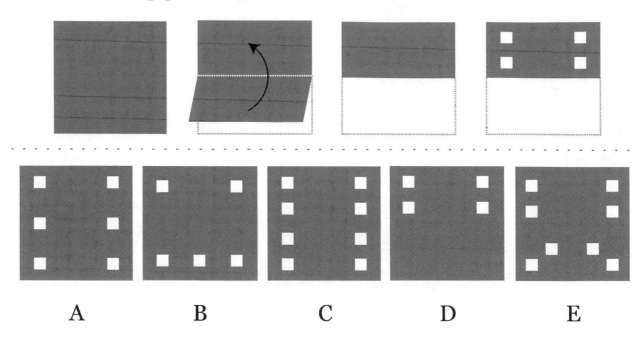

1

A   B   C   D   E

The paper in the top row is folded and cut as shown. Which paper in the bottom row is the result when the paper is unfolded?

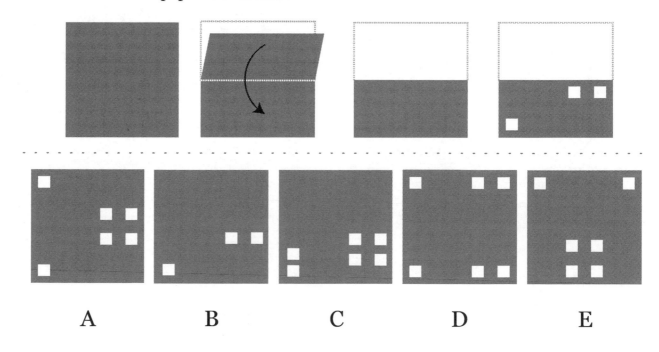

2

A   B   C   D   E

Paper Folding

The paper in the top row is folded and cut as shown. Which paper in the bottom row is the result when the paper is unfolded?

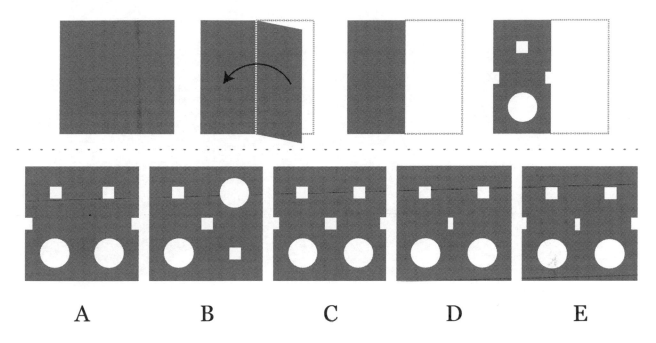

3

A   B   C   D   E

The paper in the top row is folded and cut as shown. Which paper in the bottom row is the result when the paper is unfolded?

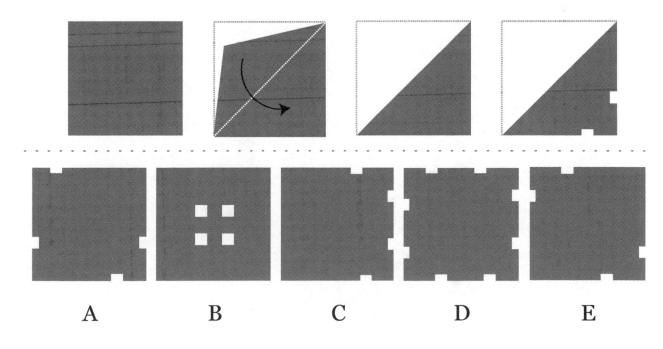

4

A   B   C   D   E

Paper Folding

The paper in the top row is folded and cut as shown. Which paper in the bottom row is the result when the paper is unfolded?

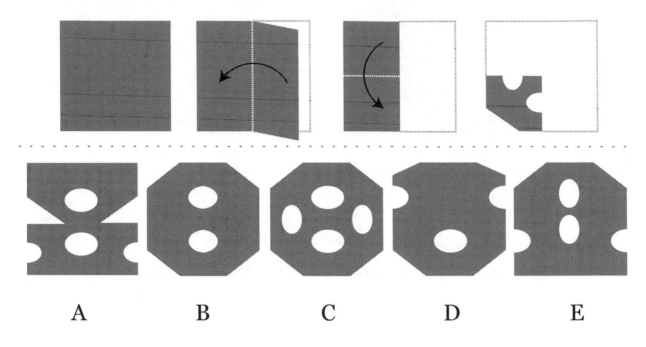

5

A   B   C   D   E

The paper in the top row is folded and cut as shown. Which paper in the bottom row is the result when the paper is unfolded?

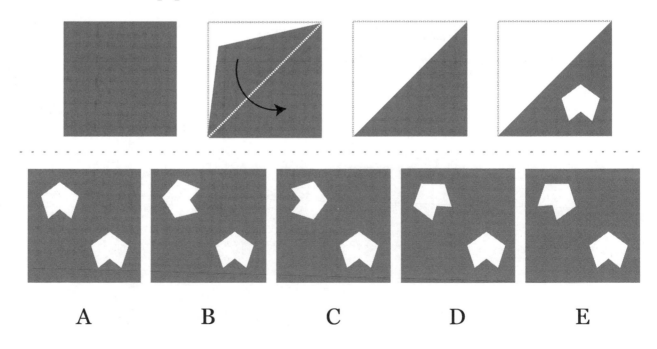

6

A   B   C   D   E

Paper Folding

The paper in the top row is folded and cut as shown. Which paper in the bottom row is the result when the paper is unfolded?

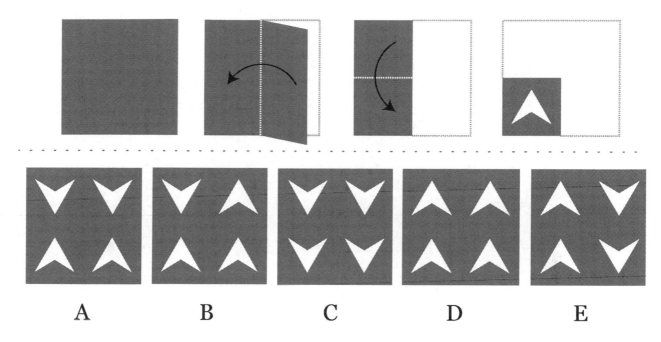

7

The paper in the top row is folded and cut as shown. Which paper in the bottom row is the result when the paper is unfolded?

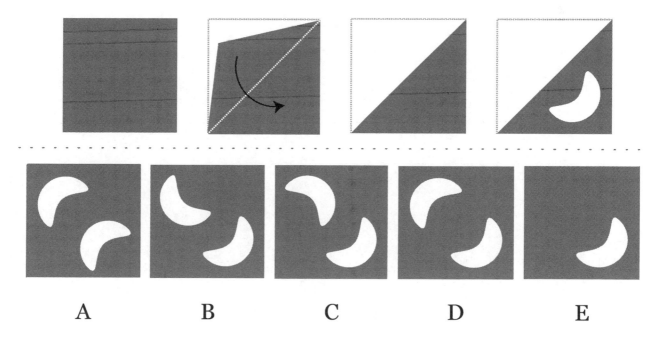

8

Paper Folding

The paper in the top row is folded and cut as shown. Which paper in the bottom row is the result when the paper is unfolded?

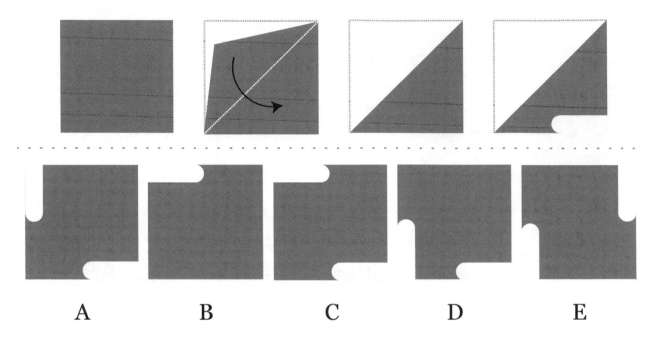

9

A	B	C	D	E

The paper in the top row is folded and cut as shown. Which paper in the bottom row is the result when the paper is unfolded?

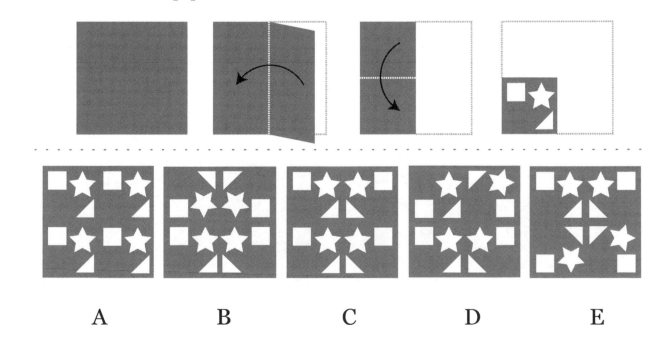

10

A	B	C	D	E

Paper Folding

The paper in the top row is folded and cut as shown. Which paper in the bottom row is the result when the paper is unfolded?

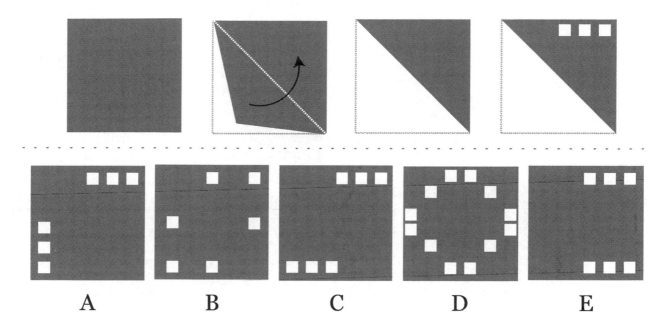

11

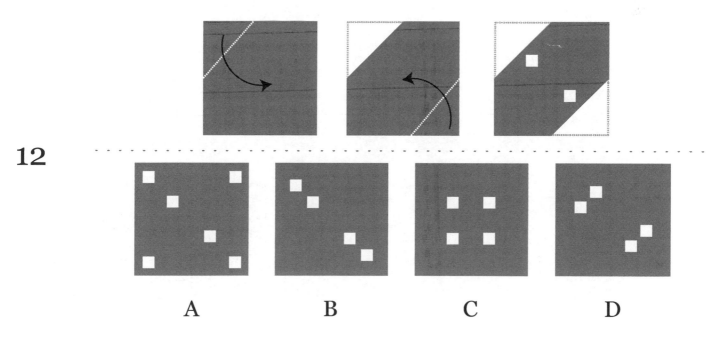

A   B   C   D   E

The paper in the top row is folded and cut as shown. Which paper in the bottom row is the result when the paper is unfolded?

12

A   B   C   D

Paper Folding

The paper in the top row is folded and cut as shown. Which paper in the bottom row is the result when the paper is unfolded?

13

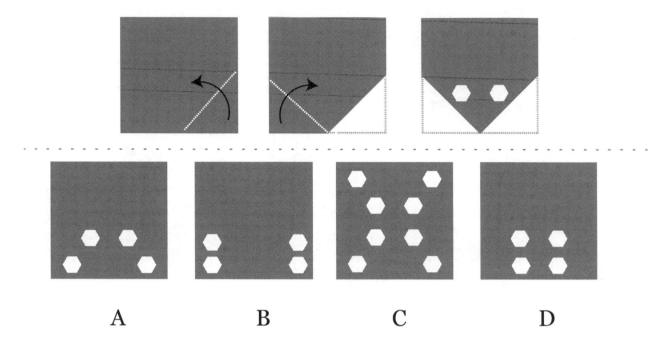

A   B   C   D

The paper in the top row is folded and cut as shown. Which paper in the bottom row is the result when the paper is unfolded?

14

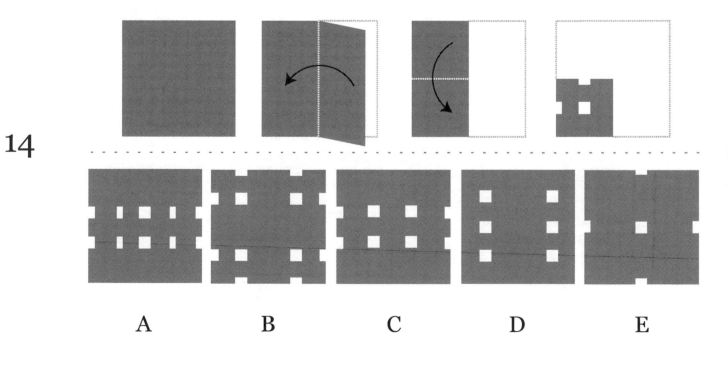

A   B   C   D   E

The paper in the top row is folded and cut as shown. Which paper in the bottom row is the result when the paper is unfolded?

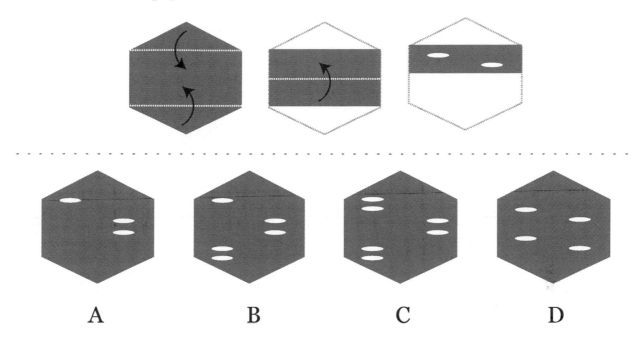

15

A   B   C   D

The paper in the top row is folded and cut as shown. Which paper in the bottom row is the result when the paper is unfolded?

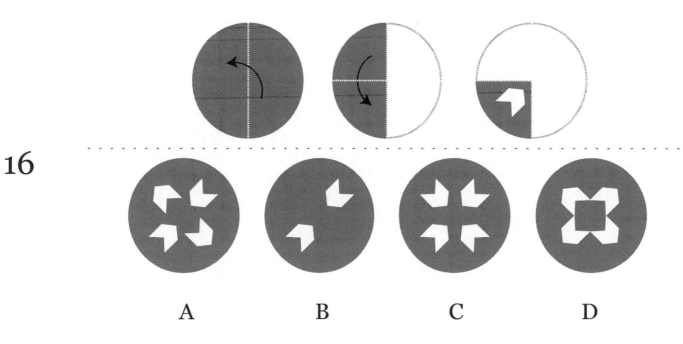

16

A   B   C   D

QUANTITATIVE BATTERY

• • • • • • • • • •

NUMBER ANALOGIES

• • • • • • • • • • • • • • • • • • • •

For each item, the student is presented with two sets of numbers.

The student needs to find the relationship between the numbers in the first set and between the numbers in the second set. Then the student needs to choose a number from the answer choices which follows the same pattern when paired with the number in the third set.

NUMBER ANALOGIES

1. [2 → 4]   [1 → 2]   [0 → ?]

    A. 2   **B.** 5   **C.** 0   **D.** 4   **E.** 1

2. [10 → 9]   [6 → 5]   [12 → ?]

    A. 11   **B.** 1   **C.** 10   **D.** 5   **E.** 13

3. [21 → 10]   [31 → 20]   [41 → ?]

    A. 20   **B.** 30   **C.** 52   **D.** 14   **E.** 40

4. [8 → 2]   [12 → 3]   [16 → ?]

    A. 3   **B.** 4   **C.** 8   **D.** 12   **E.** 16

5. [10 → 2]   [20 → 4]   [30 → ?]

    A. 3   **B.** 7   **C.** 6   **D.** 4   **E.** 10

6. [16 → 33]   [21 → 38]   [33 → ?]

    A. 33   **B.** 60   **C.** 50   **D.** 38   **E.** 51

7. [11 → 18]   [1 → 8]   [9 → ?]

    A. 54   **B.** 15   **C.** 7   **D.** 16   **E.** 12

8. [6 → 60]   [60 → 600]   [600 → ?]

    A. 10   **B.** 6   **C.** 60   **D.** 60,000   **E.** 6,000

9. [3 → 15]   [10 → 50]   [5 → ?]

    A. 35   **B.** 60   **C.** 30   **D.** 100   **E.** 25

10. [6 → 2]   [18 → 6]   [36 → ?]

    A. 11   **B.** 4   **C.** 6   **D.** 8   **E.** 12

NUMBER ANALOGIES

11. [45 → 45]   [100 → 100]   [0 → ?]

   A. 100   **B.** 10   **C.** 0   **D.** 50   **E.** 45

12. [1/4 → 1/2]   [1/2 → 1]   [1 → ?]

   A. 2   **B.** ½   **C.** 2 ½   **D.** 10   **E.** 11 ½

13. [1,027 → 2]   [4,136 → 3]   [2,641 → ?]

   A. 1   **B.** 0   **C.** 4   **D.** 6   **E.** 2

14. [20 → 10]   [12 → 6]   [16 → ?]

   A. 8   **B.** 10   **C.** 9   **D.** 1   **E.** 7

15. [3 → 9]   [6 → 18]   [9 → ?]

   A. 9   **B.** 36   **C.** 3   **D.** 18   **E.** 27

16. [16 → 12]   [18 → 14]   [20 → ?]

    A. 18   **B.** 14   **C.** 13   **D.** 16   **E.** 24

17. [16 → 8]   [12 → 6]   [8 → ?]

    A. 9   **B.** 3   **C.** 2   **D.** 12   **E.** 4

18. [102 → 1]   [6,114 → 1]   [69,491 → ?]

    A. 4   **B.** 3   **C.** 0   **D.** 2   **E.** 1

QUANTITATIVE BATTERY

• • • • • • • • • • • •

NUMBER PUZZLES

• • • • • • • • • • • • • • • • • • •

For each item, the student is presented with one or more equations.

The student needs to solve the equation and choose a number from the answer choices that will replace the question mark.

NUMBER PUZZLES

1. ⬚ = **8** + **5** - **2**

   A. 12   **B.** 1   **C.** 10   **D.** 14   **E.** 11

2. ⬚ = **15** + **15**

   A. 31   **B.** 10   **C.** 0   **D.** 40   **E.** 30

3. **20** + ⬚ = **5** x **4**

   A. 5   **B.** 25   **C.** 0   **D.** 9   **E.** 20

4. **18** = **40** - **20** - **5** + **4** - ⬚

   A. 1   **B.** 12   **C.** 3   **D.** 2   **E.** 0

5. **2** x **4** = **8** x ⬚

   A. 4   **B.** 16   **C.** 2   **D.** 1   **E.** 8

6. **19** + **47** < 🔲

  A. 56   **B.** 66   **C.** 44   **D.** 70   **E.** 61

7. **6** + **5** = **13** - **7** + 🔲

  A. 4   **B.** 5   **C.** 6   **D.** 11   **E.** 20

8. 🔲 + **25** > **45**

  A. 19   **B.** 11   **C.** 21   **D.** 15   **E.** 10

9. **6** + **7** - **9** = 🔲 + **2**

  A. 2   **B.** 4   **C.** 1   **D.** 6   **E.** 15

10. **15** + 🔲 < **26**

  A. 26   **B.** 9   **C.** 11   **D.** 13   **E.** 15

NUMBER PUZZLES

11.   **22   +   18   +   6   =   18   +   12 +** ☐

   A. 26   **B.** 10   **C.** 12   **D.** 16   **E.** 18

12.   ☐ **x   5   >   99**

   A. 20   **B.** 1   **C.** 9   **D.** 5   **E.** 10

13.   **49   +   6   +   6   +   12   =** ☐

   A. 73   **B.** 77   **C.** 91   **D.** 84   **E.** 69

14.   **35   =   20   -   5   +** ☐

   A. 5   **B.** 30   **C.** 20   **D.** 25   **E.** 32

15.   **3   +   3   +   3   =   3   x** ☐

   A. 2   **B.** 3   **C.** 9   **D.** 4   **E.** 1

16. **(3 x 1) + 5 = (☐ x 1) + 5**

   A. 4   **B.** 3   **C.** 5   **D.** 0   **E.** 9

QUANTITATIVE BATTERY

• • • • • • • • • • •

NUMBER SERIES

• • • • • • • • • • • • • • • • • •

For each item, the student is presented with a series of numbers. The order of the numbers follow a rule.

The student needs to choose a number from the answer choices which follows the same rule and replace the question mark with this number.

NUMBER SERIES

1. **2**   7   **12**   **17**   **22**   **27**   ⬚

   A. 29   **B.** 37   **C.** 32   **D.** 42   **E.** 31

2. **40**   **34**   **28**   **22**   **16**   **10**   ⬚

   A. 6   **B.** 4   **C.** 16   **D.** 8   **E.** 2

3. **10**   **30**   **50**   **70**   **90**   **110**   ⬚

   A. 120   **B.** 142   **C.** 90   **D.** 135   **E.** 130

4. **0**   **½**   **1**   **1½**   **2**   **2½**   ⬚

   A. 3   **B.** ½   **C.** 3½   **D.** 2   **E.** 4

5. **0**   **8**   **0**   **12**   **0**   ⬚

   A. 13   **B.** 0   **C.** 14   **D.** 16   **E.** 32

6. **10   9   11   8   12   7   ?**

    A. 8   **B.** 17   **C.** 6   **D.** 10   **E.** 13

7. **0   10   30   60   100   150   ?**

    A. 300   **B.** 50   **C.** 0   **D.** 175   **E.** 210

8. **0   5   4   9   8   13   ?**

    A. 16   **B.** 12   **C.** 23   **D.** 7   **E.** 21

9. **0   2   6   12   20   ?   42**

    A. 28   **B.** 40   **C.** 30   **D.** 12   **E.** 22

10. **1   2   2   4   3   ?   4   8**

    A. 4   **B.** 6   **C.** 10   **D.** 12   **E.** 3

11. **32   34   36   ☐   40   42**

A. 38   B. 37   C. 40   D. 48   E. 47

12. **0   1   5   2   10   3   ☐**

A. 0   B. 15   C. 25   D. 4   E. 20

13. **0   3   5   8   10   13   ☐**

A. 18   B. 15   C. 20   D. 28   E. 8

14. **20   23   33   36   46   49   ☐**

A. 69   B. 56   C. 59   D. 52   E. 46

15. **100   98   96   94   92   90   ☐**

A. 88   B. 90   C. 86   D. 100   E. 92

16. **2   2   4   4   6   6   ?**

    A. 8   **B.** 17   **C.** 6   **D.** 10   **E.** 13

17. **12.1   11.1   10.1   9.1   8.1   7.1   ?**

    A. 6.2   **B.** 7.12   **C.** 12.5   **D.** 8.2   **E.** 6.1

18. **1   6   1   4   1   2   1   ?**

    A. 4   **B.** 8   **C.** 6   **D.** 7   **E.** 0

COGAT Level 9 Answer Explanations

VERBAL BATTERY

Verbal Analogies

1. **D.** A candle is made of wax as a window is made of glass.

2. **B.** A dog belongs to the class of vertebrates 'mammal' as a frog belongs to the class of vertebrates called "amphibians".

3. **D.** Football is played in a 'field' as tennis is played on a 'court'.

4. **B.** Cotton is a type of fabric as gold is a type of metal.

5. **E.** Sand makes up a desert habitat as water makes up a lake habitat.

6. **E.** An oar is used to steer a rowboat as a steering wheel is used to steer a car.

7. **B.** Ladybugs have spots on their bodies as tigers have stripes on their bodies.

8. **C.** 'Rein' and 'rain' are homophones like 'there' and 'their' are homophones.

9. **A.** A clock tells time as a ruler measures distance.

10. **B.** A teacher is responsible for students as doctors are responsible for patients.

11. **C.** A triangle has three sides as an octagon has eight sides.

12. **C.** 'Pear' and 'pair' are homophones as 'hare' and 'hair' are homophones.

13. **C.** Nail polish is an accessory that is worn on nails as earrings are accessories that are worn on ears.

14. **A.** The contraction 'I'm' is composed of the words 'I am' as the contraction 'you're' is composed of the words 'you are.'

15. **E.** An immature bee is a larva as an immature fly is a maggot.

16. **C.** A spider builds a web as a wasp builds a nest.

17. **C.** 'Hilarious' describes a greater degree of 'amusing' as 'devastating' describes a greater degree of 'sad'.

18. **B.** A ring is an accessory worn around a finger as a tie is an accessory worn around the neck.

19. **D.** Leopards can be described as 'swift' as snails can be described as 'slow'.

20. **A.** A comb is a tool that is used on hair like a hammer is a tool that is used on nails.

21. **E.** 'White' and 'black' are opposites like 'before' and 'after' are opposites.

22. **D.** A mansion is an extra large house and a shack is an extra small house like a yacht is an extra large boat and a dinghy is an extra small boat.

Verbal Classifications

1. **D.** The similarity among the items is that they are all punctuation marks.

2. **A.** The similarity among the items is that they are all parts of an aeroplane.

3. **E.** The similarity among the items is that they can all be common domestic pets.

4. **B.** The similarity among the items is that they are all writing utensils.

5. **D.** The similarity among the items is that they are all types of trees.

6. **C.** The similarity among the items is that they are all types of birds.

7. **E.** The similarity among the items is that they are all rooms in a house.

8. **C.** The similarity among the items is that they are all US states.

9. **C.** The similarity among the items is that they are all products that are worn on/around the ears.

10. **A.** The similarity among the items is that they are all parts of the eye.

11. **C.** The similarity among the items is that they are all types of dances.

12. **B.** The similarity among the items is that they are all quadrilaterals or shapes with four sides.

13. **C.** The similarity among the items is that they are all prepositions of position/place.

14. **A.** The similarity among the items is that they are all contractions using the word 'is.'

15. **B.** The similarity among the items is that they are all animals that hop/jump.

16. **E.** The similarity among the items is that they are all different ways for cooking food.

17. **B.** The similarity among the items is that they are all types of school subjects.

18. **E.** The similarity among the items is that they are all conjunctions.

19. **D.** The similarity among the items is that they all require electricity in order to work properly.

20. **A.** The similarity among the items is that they are all nouns (proper or common).

Sentence Completion

1. **C.** The word 'tremble' is the best word as this verb relates to something a frightened dog might do 'all over' during a thunderstorm.

2. **B.** The word 'simplify' is the best word as this verb relates to something a teacher would do when breaking down a problem into smaller parts.

3. **B.** The word 'accelerate' is the best word because the students need to 'move quickly' in order to have the science project completed by

Friday.

4. **A.** The word 'mumbling' is the best word as this adjective relates to someone who is 'speaking too quietly'.

5. **C.** The word 'healthy' is the best word as fruit and vegetables are considered nutritious and healthy to eat.

6. **E.** The word 'heavy' is the best word as it would take one man a long time to move heavy furniture by himself.

7. **C.** The word 'graceful is the best word as this adjective relates to the movements of ballerinas.

8. **B.** The word 'but' is the best word as this conjunction is used to contrast 'loved to plant flowers' and 'disliked watering them.'

9. **A.** The word 'extinct' is the best word as this adjective relates to animals that have ceased to exist over time.

10. **D.** The word 'medicine' is the best word as a pharmacist's job is to prepare and dispense medicine.

11. **B.** The word 'pencil' is the best word as graphite is a common mineral used to fill pencils.

12. **E.** The word 'recover' is the best word as someone who is 'taking medicine' is looking to return to a normal, healthy state.

13. **A.** The word 'so' is the best word as this conjunction links the cause 'I wanted to play baseball' and the effect 'I found my bat and ran to the field.'

14. **A.** The word 'pack' is the best word is it relates to a group of wolves.

15. **E.** The word 'however' is the best word as this conjunction is used to contrast 'friends love the theater' and 'I prefer the movies.'

16. **A.** The word 'majority' is the best word as it relates to most of the children who have 'all been preparing for weeks and know the material very well.'

17. **B.** The word 'earlier' is the best word as

this comparative adverb refers to the tree that blossomed before the usual or normal expected time.

18. **E.** The word 'often' is the best word as this adverb relates to something that happens frequently or many times.

19. **C.** The word 'confuses' is the best word as this verb relates to misunderstanding or wrongly understanding the information presented.

20. **C.** The word 'grateful' is the best word as this adjective relates to someone who shows appreciation or gratitude.

NONVERBAL BATTERY

Figure Matrices

1. **D.** Moving from left to right, the outer shape becomes the inner shape. In addition, the number of sides of the outer shape in the right hand box are reduced by one side compared to the left hand box.

2. **D.** The outer shape stays the same. Inner shapes become mirror images.

3. **A.** Shaded areas turn into unshaded areas.

4. **B.** Middle shape gets smaller and goes to bottom. Bottom shape gets smaller and goes to top.Top shape gets larger and goes to middle.

5. **A.** Inner shape and outer shape each add one side.

6. **A.** Flip shape to mirror image. Add same shape to create circle but with shading opposite side.

7. **D.** Turn shape 180 degrees (1/2 turn in a clockwise direction twice).

8. **C.** In the top boxes, moving from left to right, 3 of the shapes (circles) become 1 larger outer shape (circle), which changes color, and 1 inner shape (circle), which remains the same color as original, but is slightly larger than the original).

The other 3 shapes (squares) stay the same color, but are reflected aacross the horizontal axis and are slightly smaller.In the bottom boxes, moving from left to right, 3 of the shapes (triangles) become 1 larger outer shape (triangle), which changes color, and 1 inner shape (triangle), which remains the same color as original, but is slightly larger than the original). The other 3 shapes (rectangles) stay the same color, but are reflected aacross the horizontal axis and are slightly smaller.

9. **D.** Large outer shape changes from 3D to 2D. Inner shape moves to opposite corner (top) and changes color.

10. **B.** Inner shape changes to new shape, and moves from middle positions to outer corner edges (top left, bottom right). Diagonal stripes move in a different direction.

11. **B.** Number of shapes doubles. Shapes change colors.

12. **D.** Two large shapes flip to create new shape and change color. Smaller shapes on outside of larger shapes flip and change color.

13. **D.** Middle shape becomes 2 shapes and moves to the top and bottom (same color as original). Top and bottom shape become 1 middle shape (same color as original).

14. **A.** Outer shape and arrow turn 1/4 turn clockwise.

15. **B.** Shapes merge and rotate 180 degrees.

16. **B.** Shape flips 180 degrees and inside shapes change color.

17. **B.** Left box on left is a 'close up' of the patterned side of the 3-D box on the right.

18. **A.** Turns counterclockwise 1/4 turn. The black shape at end of arrow changes to white. Two arrows move so arrows are stepped in relation to each other.

19. **D.** The exterior shape stays the same. Interior lines and shapes move counter clockwise 45 degrees.

20. **D.** Top half goes to bottom. Bottom half goes to top.

Figure Classifications

1. **B.** Figures with six sides.

2. **C.** Figures with 3 shapes

3. **A.** Four sided shapes with two parts shaded the same color, and two parts shaded another color.

4. **D.** Two arrows with right angles

5. **C.** Shapes with odd numbers of sides.

6. **C.** All shapes have 4 colors or patterns

7. **A.** Shapes with even number sides are shaded black. Shapes with odd number of sides are filled with white.

8. **B.** Only 2-D shapes

9. **C.** Figures with 5 sides.

10. **C.** Inner shape shaded black. Outer shape white.

11. **C.** One part shaded black and one part shaded white. Inner shape different than outer shape.

12. **D.** Arrows pointing opposite (180 degrees).

13. **D.** Shapes with even numbers of sides

14. **C.** Figures with 5 shapes that includes squares, rectangles and triangles.

15. **C.** Shape with diagonal pattern upwards from left to right

16. **A.** Each rectangular figure has 2 dots inside.

17. **D.** Three vertical stripes

18. **B.** Same size white arrow.

19. **B.** Diamond shape. Quadrant shadings are white, black vertical stripes, circles.

20. **A.** Four lines.

Paper Folding

1. **C**
2. **A**
3. **C**
4. **E**
5. **C**
6. **C**
7. **A**
8. **D**
9. **A**
10. **B**
11. **A**
12. **B**
13. **A**
14. **B**
15. **C**
16. **C**

QUANTITATIVE BATTERY

Number Analogies

1. **C.** Multiply by 2
2. **A.** Subtract 1
3. **B.** Subtract 11
4. **B.** Divide by 4
5. **C.** Divide by 5
6. **C.** Add 17
7. **D.** Add 7
8. **E.** Multiply by 10
9. **E.** Multiply by 5

10. **E.** Divide by 3

11. **C.** Equal to

12. **A.** Double or Multiply by 2

13. **C.** Place Value: tens place

14. **A.** Half Of or Divide by 2

15. **E.** Multiply by 3

16. **D.** Subtract 4

17. **E.** Divide by 2

18. **A.** Place value: hundreds place

Number Puzzles

1. **E.** $11 = 8 + 5 - 2$

2. **E.** $30 = 15 + 15$

3. **C.** $20 + 0 = 5 \times 4$

4. **A.** $18 = 40 - 20 - 5 + 4 - 1$

5. **D.** $2 \times 4 = 8 \times 1$

6. **D.** $19 + 47 < 70$

7. **B.** $6 + 5 = 13 - 7 + 5$

8. **C.** $21 + 25 > 45$

9. **A.** $6 + 7 - 9 = 2 + 2$

10. **B.** $15 + 9 < 26$

11. **D.** $22 + 18 + 6 = 18 + 12 + 16$

12. **A.** $20 \times 5 > 99$

13. **A.** $49 + 6 + 6 + 12 = 73$

14. **C.** $35 = 20 - 5 + 20$

15. **B.** $3 + 3 + 3 = 3 \times 3$

16. **B.** $(3 \times 1) + 5 = (3 \times 1) + 5$

Number Series

1. **C.** Add 5 to each term in the series.

2. **B.** Subtract 6 from each term in the series.

3. **E.** Add 20 to each term in the series.

4. **A.** Add ½ to each term in the series.

5. **D.** The 1st, 3rd, 5th terms in the series, etc (the odd terms) are zeroes. The other terms in the series, (2nd,4th, 6th, etc -the even terms), add 4.

6. **E.** The 1st, 3rd, 5th terms in the series, etc (the odd terms) add 1. The other terms in the series, (2nd,4th, 6th, etc -the even terms),subtract 1.

7. **E.** Each term adds 10, 20, 30, 40, etc., progressively.

8. **B.** Alternatively add five or subtract one.

9. **C.** Each term adds 2, 4, 6, 8, etc., progressively.

10. **B.** The 1st, 3rd, 5th, 7th terms in the series, etc (the odd terms) add 1. The other terms in the series, (2nd,4th, 6th, etc - the even terms), add 2.

11. **A.** Add 2 to each term in the series.

12. **B.** The 1st, 3rd, 5th terms in the series, etc. (the odd terms) add 5. The other terms in the series, (2nd, 4th, 6th, etc. - the even terms),add 1.

13. **B.** Alternatively add 3 and add 2.

14. **C.** Alternatively add 3 and add 10.

15. **A.** Subtract 2 from each term in the series.

16. **A.** Alternatively add 0 and add 2.

17. **E.** Subtract 1 from each term in the series. The decimal does not change this pattern.

18. **E.** The 1st, 3rd, 5th terms in the series, etc. (the odd terms) are equal (or add zero). For the other terms in the series (the 2nd, 4th, 6th, etc. - the even terms) subtract 2.

CogAT® Verbal Battery

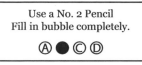

Use a No. 2 Pencil
Fill in bubble completely.
Ⓐ ● Ⓒ Ⓓ

Name:_____   Date:_____

1. Ⓐ Ⓑ Ⓒ Ⓓ Ⓔ	1. Ⓐ Ⓑ Ⓒ Ⓓ Ⓔ	1. Ⓐ Ⓑ Ⓒ Ⓓ Ⓔ
2. Ⓐ Ⓑ Ⓒ Ⓓ Ⓔ	2. Ⓐ Ⓑ Ⓒ Ⓓ Ⓔ	2. Ⓐ Ⓑ Ⓒ Ⓓ Ⓔ
3. Ⓐ Ⓑ Ⓒ Ⓓ Ⓔ	3. Ⓐ Ⓑ Ⓒ Ⓓ Ⓔ	3. Ⓐ Ⓑ Ⓒ Ⓓ Ⓔ
4. Ⓐ Ⓑ Ⓒ Ⓓ Ⓔ	4. Ⓐ Ⓑ Ⓒ Ⓓ Ⓔ	4. Ⓐ Ⓑ Ⓒ Ⓓ Ⓔ
5. Ⓐ Ⓑ Ⓒ Ⓓ Ⓔ	5. Ⓐ Ⓑ Ⓒ Ⓓ Ⓔ	5. Ⓐ Ⓑ Ⓒ Ⓓ Ⓔ
6. Ⓐ Ⓑ Ⓒ Ⓓ Ⓔ	6. Ⓐ Ⓑ Ⓒ Ⓓ Ⓔ	6. Ⓐ Ⓑ Ⓒ Ⓓ Ⓔ
7. Ⓐ Ⓑ Ⓒ Ⓓ Ⓔ	7. Ⓐ Ⓑ Ⓒ Ⓓ Ⓔ	7. Ⓐ Ⓑ Ⓒ Ⓓ Ⓔ
8. Ⓐ Ⓑ Ⓒ Ⓓ Ⓔ	8. Ⓐ Ⓑ Ⓒ Ⓓ Ⓔ	8. Ⓐ Ⓑ Ⓒ Ⓓ Ⓔ
9. Ⓐ Ⓑ Ⓒ Ⓓ Ⓔ	9. Ⓐ Ⓑ Ⓒ Ⓓ Ⓔ	9. Ⓐ Ⓑ Ⓒ Ⓓ Ⓔ
10. Ⓐ Ⓑ Ⓒ Ⓓ Ⓔ	10. Ⓐ Ⓑ Ⓒ Ⓓ Ⓔ	10. Ⓐ Ⓑ Ⓒ Ⓓ Ⓔ
11. Ⓐ Ⓑ Ⓒ Ⓓ Ⓔ	11. Ⓐ Ⓑ Ⓒ Ⓓ Ⓔ	11. Ⓐ Ⓑ Ⓒ Ⓓ Ⓔ
12. Ⓐ Ⓑ Ⓒ Ⓓ Ⓔ	12. Ⓐ Ⓑ Ⓒ Ⓓ Ⓔ	12. Ⓐ Ⓑ Ⓒ Ⓓ Ⓔ
13. Ⓐ Ⓑ Ⓒ Ⓓ Ⓔ	13. Ⓐ Ⓑ Ⓒ Ⓓ Ⓔ	13. Ⓐ Ⓑ Ⓒ Ⓓ Ⓔ
14. Ⓐ Ⓑ Ⓒ Ⓓ Ⓔ	14. Ⓐ Ⓑ Ⓒ Ⓓ Ⓔ	14. Ⓐ Ⓑ Ⓒ Ⓓ Ⓔ
15. Ⓐ Ⓑ Ⓒ Ⓓ Ⓔ	15. Ⓐ Ⓑ Ⓒ Ⓓ Ⓔ	15. Ⓐ Ⓑ Ⓒ Ⓓ Ⓔ
16. Ⓐ Ⓑ Ⓒ Ⓓ Ⓔ	16. Ⓐ Ⓑ Ⓒ Ⓓ Ⓔ	16. Ⓐ Ⓑ Ⓒ Ⓓ Ⓔ
17. Ⓐ Ⓑ Ⓒ Ⓓ Ⓔ	17. Ⓐ Ⓑ Ⓒ Ⓓ Ⓔ	17. Ⓐ Ⓑ Ⓒ Ⓓ Ⓔ
18. Ⓐ Ⓑ Ⓒ Ⓓ Ⓔ	18. Ⓐ Ⓑ Ⓒ Ⓓ Ⓔ	18. Ⓐ Ⓑ Ⓒ Ⓓ Ⓔ
19. Ⓐ Ⓑ Ⓒ Ⓓ Ⓔ	19. Ⓐ Ⓑ Ⓒ Ⓓ Ⓔ	19. Ⓐ Ⓑ Ⓒ Ⓓ Ⓔ
20. Ⓐ Ⓑ Ⓒ Ⓓ Ⓔ	20. Ⓐ Ⓑ Ⓒ Ⓓ Ⓔ	20. Ⓐ Ⓑ Ⓒ Ⓓ Ⓔ
21. Ⓐ Ⓑ Ⓒ Ⓓ Ⓔ		
22. Ⓐ Ⓑ Ⓒ Ⓓ Ⓔ		

CogAT® Nonverbal Battery

Use a No. 2 Pencil
Fill in bubble completely.
Ⓐ ● Ⓒ Ⓓ

Name:_____ Date:_____

1. Ⓐ Ⓑ Ⓒ Ⓓ	1. Ⓐ Ⓑ Ⓒ Ⓓ	1. Ⓐ Ⓑ Ⓒ Ⓓ Ⓔ
2. Ⓐ Ⓑ Ⓒ Ⓓ	2. Ⓐ Ⓑ Ⓒ Ⓓ	2. Ⓐ Ⓑ Ⓒ Ⓓ Ⓔ
3. Ⓐ Ⓑ Ⓒ Ⓓ	3. Ⓐ Ⓑ Ⓒ Ⓓ	3. Ⓐ Ⓑ Ⓒ Ⓓ Ⓔ
4. Ⓐ Ⓑ Ⓒ Ⓓ	4. Ⓐ Ⓑ Ⓒ Ⓓ	4. Ⓐ Ⓑ Ⓒ Ⓓ Ⓔ
5. Ⓐ Ⓑ Ⓒ Ⓓ	5. Ⓐ Ⓑ Ⓒ Ⓓ	5. Ⓐ Ⓑ Ⓒ Ⓓ Ⓔ
6. Ⓐ Ⓑ Ⓒ Ⓓ	6. Ⓐ Ⓑ Ⓒ Ⓓ	6. Ⓐ Ⓑ Ⓒ Ⓓ Ⓔ
7. Ⓐ Ⓑ Ⓒ Ⓓ	7. Ⓐ Ⓑ Ⓒ Ⓓ	7. Ⓐ Ⓑ Ⓒ Ⓓ Ⓔ
8. Ⓐ Ⓑ Ⓒ Ⓓ	8. Ⓐ Ⓑ Ⓒ Ⓓ	8. Ⓐ Ⓑ Ⓒ Ⓓ Ⓔ
9. Ⓐ Ⓑ Ⓒ Ⓓ	9. Ⓐ Ⓑ Ⓒ Ⓓ	9. Ⓐ Ⓑ Ⓒ Ⓓ Ⓔ
10. Ⓐ Ⓑ Ⓒ Ⓓ	10. Ⓐ Ⓑ Ⓒ Ⓓ	10. Ⓐ Ⓑ Ⓒ Ⓓ Ⓔ
11. Ⓐ Ⓑ Ⓒ Ⓓ	11. Ⓐ Ⓑ Ⓒ Ⓓ	11. Ⓐ Ⓑ Ⓒ Ⓓ Ⓔ
12. Ⓐ Ⓑ Ⓒ Ⓓ	12. Ⓐ Ⓑ Ⓒ Ⓓ	12. Ⓐ Ⓑ Ⓒ Ⓓ
13. Ⓐ Ⓑ Ⓒ Ⓓ	13. Ⓐ Ⓑ Ⓒ Ⓓ	13. Ⓐ Ⓑ Ⓒ Ⓓ
14. Ⓐ Ⓑ Ⓒ Ⓓ	14. Ⓐ Ⓑ Ⓒ Ⓓ	14. Ⓐ Ⓑ Ⓒ Ⓓ Ⓔ
15. Ⓐ Ⓑ Ⓒ Ⓓ	15. Ⓐ Ⓑ Ⓒ Ⓓ	15. Ⓐ Ⓑ Ⓒ Ⓓ
16. Ⓐ Ⓑ Ⓒ Ⓓ	16. Ⓐ Ⓑ Ⓒ Ⓓ	16. Ⓐ Ⓑ Ⓒ Ⓓ
17. Ⓐ Ⓑ Ⓒ Ⓓ	17. Ⓐ Ⓑ Ⓒ Ⓓ	
18. Ⓐ Ⓑ Ⓒ Ⓓ	18. Ⓐ Ⓑ Ⓒ Ⓓ	
19. Ⓐ Ⓑ Ⓒ Ⓓ	19. Ⓐ Ⓑ Ⓒ Ⓓ	
20. Ⓐ Ⓑ Ⓒ Ⓓ	20. Ⓐ Ⓑ Ⓒ Ⓓ	

CogAT® Quantitative Battery

Use a No. 2 Pencil
Fill in bubble completely.

Ⓐ ● Ⓒ Ⓓ

Name:_____ Date:_____

1. Ⓐ Ⓑ Ⓒ Ⓓ Ⓔ	1. Ⓐ Ⓑ Ⓒ Ⓓ Ⓔ	1. Ⓐ Ⓑ Ⓒ Ⓓ Ⓔ
2. Ⓐ Ⓑ Ⓒ Ⓓ Ⓔ	2. Ⓐ Ⓑ Ⓒ Ⓓ Ⓔ	2. Ⓐ Ⓑ Ⓒ Ⓓ Ⓔ
3. Ⓐ Ⓑ Ⓒ Ⓓ Ⓔ	3. Ⓐ Ⓑ Ⓒ Ⓓ Ⓔ	3. Ⓐ Ⓑ Ⓒ Ⓓ Ⓔ
4. Ⓐ Ⓑ Ⓒ Ⓓ Ⓔ	4. Ⓐ Ⓑ Ⓒ Ⓓ Ⓔ	4. Ⓐ Ⓑ Ⓒ Ⓓ Ⓔ
5. Ⓐ Ⓑ Ⓒ Ⓓ Ⓔ	5. Ⓐ Ⓑ Ⓒ Ⓓ Ⓔ	5. Ⓐ Ⓑ Ⓒ Ⓓ Ⓔ
6. Ⓐ Ⓑ Ⓒ Ⓓ Ⓔ	6. Ⓐ Ⓑ Ⓒ Ⓓ Ⓔ	6. Ⓐ Ⓑ Ⓒ Ⓓ Ⓔ
7. Ⓐ Ⓑ Ⓒ Ⓓ Ⓔ	7. Ⓐ Ⓑ Ⓒ Ⓓ Ⓔ	7. Ⓐ Ⓑ Ⓒ Ⓓ Ⓔ
8. Ⓐ Ⓑ Ⓒ Ⓓ Ⓔ	8. Ⓐ Ⓑ Ⓒ Ⓓ Ⓔ	8. Ⓐ Ⓑ Ⓒ Ⓓ Ⓔ
9. Ⓐ Ⓑ Ⓒ Ⓓ Ⓔ	9. Ⓐ Ⓑ Ⓒ Ⓓ Ⓔ	9. Ⓐ Ⓑ Ⓒ Ⓓ Ⓔ
10. Ⓐ Ⓑ Ⓒ Ⓓ Ⓔ	10. Ⓐ Ⓑ Ⓒ Ⓓ Ⓔ	10. Ⓐ Ⓑ Ⓒ Ⓓ Ⓔ
11. Ⓐ Ⓑ Ⓒ Ⓓ Ⓔ	11. Ⓐ Ⓑ Ⓒ Ⓓ Ⓔ	11. Ⓐ Ⓑ Ⓒ Ⓓ Ⓔ
12. Ⓐ Ⓑ Ⓒ Ⓓ Ⓔ	12. Ⓐ Ⓑ Ⓒ Ⓓ Ⓔ	12. Ⓐ Ⓑ Ⓒ Ⓓ Ⓔ
13. Ⓐ Ⓑ Ⓒ Ⓓ Ⓔ	13. Ⓐ Ⓑ Ⓒ Ⓓ Ⓔ	13. Ⓐ Ⓑ Ⓒ Ⓓ Ⓔ
14. Ⓐ Ⓑ Ⓒ Ⓓ Ⓔ	14. Ⓐ Ⓑ Ⓒ Ⓓ Ⓔ	14. Ⓐ Ⓑ Ⓒ Ⓓ Ⓔ
15. Ⓐ Ⓑ Ⓒ Ⓓ Ⓔ	15. Ⓐ Ⓑ Ⓒ Ⓓ Ⓔ	15. Ⓐ Ⓑ Ⓒ Ⓓ Ⓔ
16. Ⓐ Ⓑ Ⓒ Ⓓ Ⓔ	16. Ⓐ Ⓑ Ⓒ Ⓓ Ⓔ	16. Ⓐ Ⓑ Ⓒ Ⓓ Ⓔ
17. Ⓐ Ⓑ Ⓒ Ⓓ Ⓔ		17. Ⓐ Ⓑ Ⓒ Ⓓ Ⓔ
18. Ⓐ Ⓑ Ⓒ Ⓓ Ⓔ		18. Ⓐ Ⓑ Ⓒ Ⓓ Ⓔ

BONUS

DOWNLOAD QUANTITATIVE CHALLENGE QUESTIONS

If you also want additional quantitative challenge questions, please go to the following link to download them!

To get your challenge questions today, please visit:
https://originstutoring.lpages.co/cogat3challengequestions

Challenge questions can help a student get used to doing the most difficult questions on the test.

Get the questions now at
https://originstutoring.lpages.co/cogat3challengequestions

Made in the USA
Lexington, KY
10 July 2019